# STOP
## the
# BULLYING!

written and illustrated by
Andrew Matthews

Seashell Publishers
AUSTRALIA

**Stop the Bullying!**
Copyright © 2011 by Andrew Matthews
and Seashell Publishers

**Published by:**
Seashell Publishers,
PO Box 325, Trinity Beach,
Queensland, Australia, 4879

Tel: (within Australia) 07 4055 6966
Tel: (from outside Australia) 61 7 4055 6966
Fax: (within Australia) 07 4057 6966
Fax: (from outside Australia) 61 7 4057 6966
Email: info@seashell.com.au
Visit our website: www.seashell.com.au

Layout and design by Twocan and Seashell Publishers

ISBN 978-0-9872057-2-8

First published October 2011

Also by the same author:
*Being Happy!*
*Making Friends*
*Follow Your Heart*
*Happiness in a Nutshell*
*Being a Happy Teen*
*Happiness Now*
*Happiness in Hard Times*

## HOW THIS BOOK HAPPENED

In 2009, Julie—my wife and publisher—heard the stories of Allem Halkic and Richard Plotkin, and said, "Andrew, we have to do something. We need to write a book to help stop bullying." From that moment Julie has been the driving force behind this project. She has done research, made phone calls, jumped on planes and interviewed all the people to make this happen.

Julie is actually the co-author of *Stop the Bullying!* We wrote this book together, sentence by sentence. But Julie is too modest to take the credit she deserves and refuses to have her name on the cover.

Julie, once more, thank you my darling. You are an inspiration. You are my inspiration.

**Andrew Matthews**

### THANK YOU

Thank you to the Victorian Police, and to the Arson and Explosives Squad led by Sergeant Scott Barnes for supporting this project.

To Vicki Vassilopoulos of the Victorian Police, thank you for your continuing help and professionalism whenever we needed to speak with you.

To Leon O'Brien and Sally Gibson of the Office of the Public Advocate, thank you for taking the time to give us critical information on the Richard Plotkin case.

To Julia Schembri of Schembri and Co, thank you.

Dina and Ali Halkic, thank you for the many hours you spent with us. Your love, your drive and your courage are an inspiration.

Gordon Keane—thank you for being so open and honest in sharing your story.

Tori Matthews-Osman, thank you for sharing your experiences.

To Michelle Street, thank you for your help with research, editing and for all your help at Seashell Publishers every day.

To Stan Davis, Michele Elliot, Katie Jarvis, Helen Peuleve and Maryjane and Carlo Chiarotto; thank you for your contribution to our book. Thank you for your advice and generosity. Thank you for responding to our emails so promptly and for taking phone calls when we needed your help. To Jane Thomas, thank you for your help—again.

To Kate Halfpenny, executive editor of Who Magazine and Robin Bailey of Brisbane Radio 97.3FM, thank you for your kind assistance.

To all of you who sent us your stories from which we learnt so much, thank you. We did not have room to include all your stories in our book! And to our readers, thank you for 20 years of support and thank you for your daily emails which inspire us to keep writing.

**Julie M Matthews, Publisher**

# BULLYING AT HOME

DAD

BIG BROTHER

LITTLE BROTHER

ROCKY

ANDREW MATTHEWS

# CONTENTS

# BULLIED TO DEATH

## 1

## Cyber-Bullying: Dina and Ali Halkic tell the story of their son, Allem

The evening of Wednesday February 4, 2009, was like any other. Our son Allem had dinner with us and then went with his mate Thanh to their friend Monica's house. They spent the evening teaching Monica's little sisters to play cards.

Allem got home at around 10.30pm. He asked my wife Dina, "What's for lunch tomorrow?"

Dina said, "It's in the refrigerator."

Allem seemed bright and happy. He grabbed a bag of chips and a can of coke which he usually does to have a snack. He went to his room and shut the door.

It was almost midnight when we heard him still on his computer. I was about to get up to say, "Allem, you need to turn everything off, you've got school tomorrow." But we heard nothing more and Dina and I fell asleep.

We awoke at 6:30 next morning to find his door open. Allem's room was empty. On his bed was a note. It seemed Allem had gone to the West Gate Bridge.

Shocked, stunned, numb, we called every friend we could think of. No one knew anything. We called the police.

At 7.15am the police called back. They asked if Allem had an insulin pump with him—and asked what colour it was. We knew something was very wrong.

At 7.30am a police car pulled into our driveway but the officers sat in the car for several minutes. We could see they didn't want to get out. We stood at the front door. Dina held me so tight.

I asked the police, "Is our boy alive?

And they said, "I'm sorry, Mr Halkic. He's dead."

Allem's body had been found at the foot of the bridge. I can't describe how that moment is. Something inside you dies.

Allem was our only child and he was everything that we could have wanted in a son. He was sensitive, intelligent and unusually considerate. Allem had many friends that we knew well—they would come to our house to eat, play music and just relax.

Allem loved Metallica, loved his Ipod, playing his guitar and playing poker. He loved his Mum's potato scallops.

We were a very close, happy family. Our life revolved around Allem and his friends—we felt we were as much a part of Allem's life as parents could be.

Unable to believe or comprehend this tragedy, we asked ourselves, "What was so terribly wrong that we knew nothing about?"

## Allem in Cyberspace

Allem liked to chat with his friends on his laptop. He would talk to ten or fifteen people at a time and I would hear these beeps come out of the room. I'd come in and say, "Allem, what are all these screens popping up?"

And he would explain, "They're all my friends."

I'd ask, "How are you talking to all these people at once?"

He would shrug and smile, "We all do it."

> we asked ourselves, "What was so terribly wrong that we knew nothing about?"

We always assumed, "Our child is home with us, in his bedroom. If he is under our roof, he is always safe and he can't get hurt."

In December 2008, Allem had fallen out with a former friend. This friend, who was three years older than Allem, had made insulting comments about another of Allem's friends. The disagreement escalated.

Allem began to receive threatening texts and emails, "*Ur all mouth and no action, wait till I get my hands on you, I'm telling u now I'll put you in hospital,*"… "*Don't be surprised if you get hit sometime soon. You f_cked with the wrong person … it's payback time.*"… "*You'll know my car as I drive towards you—the white one with the spotlight on top.*" There were threats to involve well-known violent gangs.

The perpetrator also circulated emails to his friends encouraging them to gang up on Allem: "We're going to smash that 'dog'."

Allem received over 300 threatening messages on his phone and his laptop. The bullying was relentless. Dina said, "We would hear Allem bashing the keys of his computer but we didn't realise what he was doing online. We had no idea he was trying to save his own life, the poor thing!"

We never saw any sign that Allem was struggling and definitely no sign that he might ever take his life. His friend Cain said later, "Allem didn't like anything to do with conflict. It was typical he didn't want to bother his friends … he didn't have a bad bone in his body."

## The Future Allem Never Saw

During Christmas vacation 2008 Allem came to work with me for a couple of weeks—I work for an international express and logistics company and Allem's job was to pack and sort parcels. After school resumed I noticed a barcode from work stuck on his door. He explained with a grin, "Dad, every day this reminds me why I have to stay at school."

Dina and I felt so proud. Allem had applied to a college. I had chosen a car for him. Allem wanted to be a chef and travel the world on a luxury liner.

We were so thrilled when Allem was born. You hold a new born baby in your arms. You never think that seventeen years later you will hold that same child in your arms—and every bone in his body is broken. You never think that seventeen years later you will bury your beloved son in such horrific circumstances—and you will never see him again.

Eight hundred people attended Allem's funeral.

> 66 You never think that seventeen years later you will hold that same child in your arms—and every bone in his body is broken. 99

## The Curse of Suicide

It's been three years since we lost our boy to cyber-bullying. Every second is torture. There is a hole in my heart, a throbbing physical pain. Every day I hope I won't wake up. Weekends are the worst.

> 66 There is a hole in my heart, a throbbing physical pain. 99

I see a four-year-old child with his parents—in a park or a mall—and I think of Allem at four. I am happy for the parents—that they have their child. I pause to watch the child at play—and the parents probably look at me and wonder, "What are you staring at?"

I see a teenage boy—I think of Allem. Allem has a friend who dresses like him, has hair like him. He used to come to our house often, even after Allem passed away. He's a great kid—but just to see him tears my heart out. Someone who has never lost a child could never understand.

I bend to tie my shoelaces and I remember tying Allem's shoes. Everything is a reminder.

Every person has their own smell. Your child has a scent—Allem's room had the scent of Allem. When we lost him, Dina and I would just sit in his room to be with Allem's scent. It stayed for about six months—it was a comfort for us. You hold onto whatever you can.

When you lose a child you do things that make no sense—because life makes no sense. Dina still cooks for Allem every night. She washes his clothes each week. Every day I carry around a briefcase with all Allem's things in it—even the autopsy report. Allem's life is in my briefcase.

We visit Allem's grave three, four, five times a week. Do we feel better when we are there? Yes… no…I don't know.

We ask ourselves a hundred questions, over and over and over:

"What if we had watched his laptop more closely?"

"What if we had woken up in time?"

"What if we had asked more questions?…"

It is a life sentence of questions.

I hate liars—I hate people who pretend. But every day I pretend. Every day I lie. I go to the supermarket and friends ask, "How are you?"

I say, "Good".

People at work say, "How are you doing?"

I say, "Fine".

It's all a lie.

## Talk to Your Children about Death and Suicide

We never talked to Allem about death—or suicide.

If Allem only knew how much we would suffer—if he knew how many tears his mother would shed—he would never have done what he did.

If Allem only knew how his friends would be scarred for life he would never have taken his own life. But how could he know the wreckage he would leave behind? How can a teenager understand? If an adult aged 65 and terminally ill decides to end it all, he knows what he is doing. But not a teenager, not Allem.

I have friends whose children took their own lives. Like me, they never talked to their teenagers about death. Unlike me, they never talk about their children now. They never talk about suicide.

It's agony to talk about it—but we must speak up for the sake of all teenagers.

I was so naive. I used to think that bullying only happens to unpopular kids, or chubby kids or skinny kids. I used to think that suicides only happen in dysfunctional families. Now I know differently.

In our hallway we have a light. When Allem went out at night, we would leave it on for him—as many parents do. When he came in he would turn it off—and we would think: "Allem is home—and safe".

Allem's light has been burning for three years now. Allem, it will always be on for you.

## The Myth

There is a myth that bullied teenagers are misfits. The myth says that targets of bullying are depressed and loners.

But Allem Halkic was about as happy and balanced as any seventeen-year-old could be. He was as loved as any seventeen-year-old could be. But no seventeen-year-old is equipped to suffer relentless threats on his life and safety. If Allem—who was happy, balanced, fun-loving and popular—was vulnerable, then any child is vulnerable.

## Australia's First Cyber-Bullying Conviction

The perpetrator was prosecuted by Victoria Police, he pleaded guilty and was convicted. It was Australia's first cyber-bullying conviction.

Around the world, legislation is catching up with bullies. Parents and teachers should no longer dismiss bullying as "a bit of teasing and everyone does it". When children get hurt, no longer is it seen as a *bit of fun gone wrong*. Bullies are being convicted and jailed.

Allem is one of countless teens who have been pushed to the edge by bullying. Right now there are children in Chicago, Oslo, Tokyo and Manchester—and in a thousand cities in between—attempting suicide or planning it.

In western countries, suicide is now the biggest killer of our youth—more teens die from suicide than from drugs or road accidents. We tell our kids to avoid drugs, we tell our kids to drive carefully. We talk to our teens about food, fashion and football. But who is talking to our kids about suicide? Suicide is still taboo: "It doesn't happen in our house!"

We have to get the message to our children, "Bullying doesn't last forever. But suicide IS forever".

### The Halkics' fight to restore Allem's dignity

The court had found the bully guilty of a crime. But this wasn't enough for Dina and Ali Halkic. Says Ali, "People assume that if someone commits suicide he must be suffering depression. Allem was not suffering from depression." Dina and Ali set out to prove it.

They sought the help of Julia Schembri of Schembri and Company, lawyers, and jointly they took Allem's case to the Victim's of Crime Assistance Tribunal. They worked for a year on the case—and proved that Allem's suicide was the direct result of an act of violence online. It was a landmark decision, the first victory of its kind for Australia. They proved that cyber-bullying can kill.

Julia Schembri, a specialist in the field of victims of crime said, "I was compelled to make a difference for the Halkic family and to restore Allem's dignity by achieving recognition that he died as a direct result of violence online."

In a letter to the Magistrate of the Tribunal Ali said, "Your finding…has restored so much of Allem's dignity and honour. You have given my wife Dina back her pride and the feeling that she did not fail as a mother and that she should be proud of how she raised our son. You have given us a chance to live and a reason to continue because we believe changes can be made. The fight was a struggle but we understand the importance of community awareness to tackle the dangers of the cyber-world to children. What you have done for Allem will help so many others."

### The Halkic's Campaign

In spite or their daily grief, Dina and Ali Halkic have campaigned non-stop to raise awareness about online bullying and youth suicide. They speak in schools and at sports clubs, they grant media interviews on a weekly basis. They lobby government—and when big government won't listen, they lobby little government.

Dina and Ali worked with Leader Community Newspapers to launch the "Don't Hurt" campaign, where teens make a promise to tackle cyber-bullying.

Says Ali, "We can't change the world but we can change our own back yard. It's up to us to be caring people. It's up to us to make things safe for our children."

---

## THE PROMISE

*I will not join in, laugh or look on if I know cyber-bullying is happening.*

*I will not stand by and do nothing.*

*I will tell a teacher, a parent, an adult or a trusted friend if I become aware of cyber-bullying.*

*I will not respond to any bullying message or image, and I will save the evidence.*

---

Ali and Dina organised a rally for 300 people at Melbourne's West Gate Bridge—the bridge from which Allem plunged to his death, and the site of hundreds of suicides. They headed a campaign to have safety rails installed. They lobbied a government which for five years has said, "Too hard, too expensive, not worth it." They wrote to newspapers and talked to every radio station and politician that would listen. Eventually, at a cost of over ten million dollars, safety rails were installed. The result? An 85% reduction in deaths in the first year: there were 37 suicides in 2009 and 4 in 2010. In 2011? None to date.

Says Ali, "I have spent all the money I have and a lot of money I don't have on this campaign. It is too late to save my boy. We are doing this to save other children.

"By going public, we hope that we can encourage people to talk openly about suicide. If mums, dads and teenagers can discuss suicide openly, then other families don't have to go through what Dina and I have endured. Suicide is preventable."

Allem's friends uploaded a photographic tribute to YouTube and recorded this song:

*I saw my life flash before me*
*The people that I have loved*
*I saw the way that I could die one day*
*There's nothing I can do to change this*
*There's no words I can say*
*I swear I'll make the most of every single day*
*And it's my life you've abandoned forever – I've lost you*
*And it's my life you walked out on, left a trail of tears and broken faces*
*How could you throw it all away?*

Allem was a normal, happy and energetic teenager from a loving and supportive family. He had many friends and everything to live for. Allem showed no signs of distress and told no one about the cyber-bullying.

Three years after his death, some of Allem's friends wrote these messages:

Allem, not a day goes by that we don't think of you, and the wonderful memories you left behind. Brother, in times of need, never judging, always there. Please always remember you were loved like no other.
**Daniel and Cain Heffernan**

Not a day goes by that I don't think about you. It feels like it was yesterday we were having a laugh together. Love and miss you my brother.
**Rob Nguyen**

I really miss you brother and not a day goes by I don't think of you. I really wish you spoke with me for support the night you tragically passed away.
**Thanh Bui**

Growing up together as teenagers, you were the type of person to always try new things and make our days interesting, as long as we had a good time. You are the kind of mate everyone needs. It makes you who you are and the reason why we all love you. Always and forever missed, Allem. RIP.
**Eric Chau**

Allem Halkic, forever, I will love you. Not a day goes by where my heart does not ache for the fact that you are not here beside us all. My heart does still have the ability to smile, in the memory of you and your laughter.
*Sarah E. Doughty*

Not a day goes by that you aren't continuously on my mind. I miss your laugh, I miss your smile, I miss the way the room would light up as soon as you entered but most of all I just miss you. You will be in my heart, forever and always.
*Megan Portelli*

No words are beautiful enough to describe you. No words are passionate enough to describe how much we love you and there are no words to explain how much we all miss you. Allem Halkic - the brightest star shining in the sky.
*Sarah Darmanin*

Allem Halkic - I will forever be grateful that you came into my life. I have the unforgettable memories we shared locked and sealed in my heart and they will live on just as your spirit does through your parents, family and friends. You will never ever be forgotten. Forever young, forever loved and forever missed.
*Celine Creighton*

MANY TIMES WE
HAVE MISSED YOU
A MILLION TIMES
WE HAVE CRIED
IF LOVE COULD
HAVE SAVED YOU
YOU NEVER WOULD
HAVE DIED

# Bullying at School

## 2

*I am the person who sits next to you in class.*
*I am the person who is a bit overweight.*
*I am the person who is laughed at because I am short.*
*I am the person who is picked on because I like computers.*
*I am the person who talks with an accent.*
*I am the person who isn't great at gym.*
*I am the person who is always to blame.*
*I am the person who takes the bus home in fear.*
*I am the person who stumbles when I walk too fast.*
*But I am also the person who is brave enough to wake up and do it again the next day.*

**Nigel Potts**

---

## "What's Wrong with Me?"

**M**ATTHEW'S STORY: I am a divorced man in my 40s who was bullied constantly for three years, grades 7 through 9. I lived in horror of gym days, which were three days a week. I slept with my bare feet outside of the covers in the winter to make myself sick. I ran the thermometer under warm water. I went to the bathroom (at home) and took the toilet bowl scrubber and stirred up my waste. Then I called my Mom in and said, "Look Mom. I can't go to school today because I have diarrhea."

I have been treated for and/or am on medication for major depression, obsessive-compulsive disorder, social anxiety, general anxiety, and post-traumatic stress. Sometimes death seems to be the only answer. I have an obsessive thought, "I was raped as a child and nobody came to my funeral," meaning, it killed me and nobody cared. Also high on the list of recurring thoughts is "WHAT'S WRONG WITH ME?" and "WHY DON'T PEOPLE LIKE ME?"

I am on four drugs for depression and anxiety. The doctors want to keep me sedated so I won't kill myself, which would make them look bad, although they

> **66 Here it is 30 years since we moved away from the bully and he still controls my life. 99**

won't admit it. None of my psychiatrists or psychologists has dealt with my abuse as a child because it is easier for them to say everything is the depression, write a prescription, and show me to the door. My next plan is to get into group therapy or some kind of support group.

But pills will never stop the depression until the abuse issues have healed more. The pills are not helping me to function. Here it is 30 years since we moved away from the bully and he still controls my life. I want my life back. I am tired of being a freak.

Parents and teachers will sometimes dismiss bullying as "normal" or *kids having harmless fun*. That isn't Matthew's experience.

### "We Know What Happens in our School"

In 2000 two Canadian researchers—Craig and Pepler—set out to discover how much teachers really knew about the bullying that happened in their school. They planted hidden microphones and cameras in classrooms and playgrounds. What did they find?

*"Our observations indicate that teachers intervene in 14% of classroom episodes and only 4% of playground episodes of bullying."* [1]

They confirm what you already know— there aren't enough teachers to know all that is happening. This would explain the other finding: when asked whether teachers almost always intervene to stop bullying: *71% of teachers said "Yes" but only 25% of students said "Yes".*

### When a Child is Bullied

Bullied children are likely to:
- skip school
- develop eating disorders
- suffer poor health

ANDREW MATTHEWS

- suffer depression
- become vandals and shoplifters
- abuse drugs and alcohol
- perform poorly at school. Bullied children are so distracted, so intent on avoiding further bullying, so busy concocting excuses to avoid school, how can they possibly perform?

Words can hurt the most. An 84-year-old man who wrote to Kidscape in the UK said, "I can remember every word those fiends said. I've been hearing their bullying jeers all my life." Cruel remarks remain carved into our memories long after the pain of a thrashing has disappeared.

Some bullied children seek revenge. Research into 37 school shooting incidents in the USA involving 41 different attackers between 1974 and 2000 revealed that 71% of the attackers "felt bullied, persecuted or injured by others prior to the attack": 2

- Charles Andrew Williams was a high school freshman in Santee California. Fellow students made fun of his big ears and his frail body. His older brother Michael remembers, "He has big ears and he's real skinny. People like to pick on him. It was like that as long as I can remember". They called him Anorexic Andy. His friend Neil O'Grady said, "He was always getting picked on. He's scrawny, he's little. People think he's dumb."

    One day Andy snapped. He took a gun to school and killed two students and wounded another thirteen people.

- Eric Harris and Dylan Klebold were relentlessly bullied and ostracised at Columbine High School in Littleton, Colorado. In one incident they were falsely accused by a classmate of bringing marijuana to school—prompting a search of their property. In another incident an onlooker recalls their humiliation, "People surrounded them in the commons and squirted ketchup packets all over them, calling them faggots. That happened while teachers watched. They couldn't fight back. They wore the ketchup all day and went home covered with it."

    In 1999 Harris and Klebold used home-made pipe bombs and automatic weapons to massacre 12 students and a teacher. Twenty-four-people were wounded.  A suicide note left by Eric indicated it was "payback time".

    As one student who lived through the terrifying incident in the school library observed, "THEY WANTED US TO FEEL THEIR PAIN."

*I don't want to die but it is the only way to end the pain.*

## Suicide

We could list a thousand children here—children like Jeffrey Johnston, 15, from Florida, USA, Chanelle Rae, 14, from Geelong, Australia, Marie Bentham, 8 from Manchester, UK, Akiko Uemura, 12 from Honshu, Japan—bright, beautiful kids who were bullied into suicide.

We might ask, "What could be worse than dying? Why would a child commit suicide to avoid being beaten up? It makes no sense."

It is the relentlessness—continual texts, taunts, beatings—and never knowing what will happen next. It is the embarrassment, humiliation and shame. After months of sleepless nights, a teenager, seeing no way out and feeling totally alone sometimes says, "I can't stand this any more. Anything is better than this. Death is better than this". Again and again, the message from those who have taken their own lives—and the message from those who have attempted suicide—is, "I didn't want to die but there was no other way to end this pain".

It has nothing to do with logic. If prisoners of war who are continually threatened and sleep-deprived become confused and a little crazy, what can we expect of a child?

**In a Nutshell**
Of course a bullied child doesn't think straight!

## "My Kids Would Tell Me!"

Dawn-Marie Wesley, 14, of Mission, B.C wrote in her suicide note, "If I try to get help it will get worse. They are always looking for a new person to beat up and they are the toughest girls. If I ratted they would get suspended and there would be no stopping them..."

Dawn-Marie chose to suffer in silence. You say, "If my kids were being bullied I would know. They would tell me if they were suffering". Would they?

> 66 *If I ratted they would get suspended and there would be no stopping them...* 99

## Reasons Why Kids Don't Tell Their Parents

Imagine that your twelve-year-old son Marcus is being bullied. His classmates throw his homework in the river, they kick him in the schoolyard, steal his money, they call him "Loser".

Statistics tell us that there is ONE CHANCE IN TEN that Marcus will tell you about it—and only ONE IN TWENTY he would tell his teacher.

Why does a suffering child keep such a secret from loving parents? Let Marcus tell you why:

**"The Bullying Would Get Worse!** If my Dad spoke to the bullies OR their parents, I would become a joke. The bullies would get meaner!"

Kids get bullied when they aren't cool. And the least cool thing in the universe is to have your uncool parents interfering. So the bullied teen thinks, "If I am already being bullied for being UNCOOL, what will the bullies do when they see how UNCOOL my parents are!"

**"My Parents Would Be Ashamed of Me.** I don't want my parents to think I'm a loser and that everybody hates me. I don't want them to think I can't handle it. My mother already tells me how to live! If she knew about the bullying, they would be impossible!"

Bullied children believe they are partly to blame: "If I wasn't such a nerd, people wouldn't make fun of me." "If I didn't wear such stupid clothes, kids would leave me alone." "If I wasn't so ugly, skinny, fat, dumb, kids wouldn't beat me up."

Marcus also doesn't want you to be ashamed, "My son is a dork!"

**"My Parents Would Embarrass Me.** They might visit the principal. I would rather die than have my parents come and talk to the teachers. I would look so stupid—I would be the laughing stock of the whole school."

A teenager's main goal in life is to appear cool and in control—so the last thing he wants is parents interfering. Parents are embarrassing enough already!

**"My Parents Would Want to Control Me.** They are always telling me what to do now. If they knew what trouble I am in, they would be telling me what to wear, criticising my friends, my clothes ..."

**"It's Not Right to Rat, Snitch, Tattle."** Children learn that it is not right to rat on a bully. Young ones of eight or ten may still feel that it is okay to tell an adult—but by the time they are teenagers they are well and truly conditioned to suffer in silence. Boys especially learn that you have to shut up and take it like a man.

**"It's Just a Part of Growing Up."** Many children—and adults—have come to believe that bullying is just a part of growing up and no one can help them. This is old-fashioned thinking.

Above are SIX very good reasons for children to suffer in silence. And here is the problem: they only need ONE good reason.

## Cyber-Bullying: More Reasons Why Kids Don't Tell Their Parents

*"The internet and puberty do not mix!"*
   **Malinda Wilson, Seattle Police Department**

Fourteen-year-old Mary is being cyber-bullied. Mary's classmates have created a web page featuring her photograph called "Ugly Mary". They send her anonymous emails saying, "You're a pig. Lose some weight!" They bombard her with text messages that read "Go kill yourself!" Would Mary tell her parents?

She probably won't for the reasons we discussed earlier. And with cyber-bullying, there are more reasons:

**"My Laptop is my Life.** If I told my mother about the bullying, she might confiscate it—together with my phone! I would be a total outcast!

"If kids are spreading nasty rumours about me, I need to know what they are. Better to be bullied and be in touch than to be bullied and not know what kids are saying about you.

MATTHEWS

"Being bullied is hell but being cut off would be worse. Email and texting is how I connect. I couldn't live without Facebook."

If you are over forty, your computer is probably just a tool—maybe essential but still a tool. For Mary, it is her life. You decorate your lounge room, she decorates her page on Facebook. You visit cyberspace. She lives there.

**"My Parents Would Want to Monitor Everything.** My parents would freak if they saw some of the chatrooms I visit and some of the emails I write! Better to suffer the harassment than have my parents looking over my shoulder every minute."

So here are EIGHT very good reasons for Mary to suffer in silence.

And she only needs ONE.

**DANNII:** Dannii Sanders was an Australian trampoline champion who represented her country in Japan in 2010. Dannii was popular, bubbly and vivacious. Said her Mum, Christine, "She was blonde with blue eyes, almost like purple, and they sparkled when she was happy. She would eat and sleep and dance to music videos and bounce on her trampoline."

Dannii had nearly 2,000 friends on Facebook. And she was cyber-bullied.

In July 2011, as a result of online bullying and struggles within herself, she committed suicide. Danni's death caused a wave of grief amongst hundreds of friends in Sydney. Her mother said, "I don't believe she wanted to die."

Was Facebook the cause of Danni's death? "No", say her parents. It was more complicated than that.

## What are Real Friends?

Here's what we do know: teenagers with thousands of buddies in cyberspace can be just as lonely as teenagers with none. You might have an army of acquaintances on the internet—but how many of them would cross the road to help you when you really need them? How many of them would even recognise you in the street?

My friend Tony has four children. When he discovered that Julie and I were writing a book on bullying, he asked, "What about cyber-bullying? I've got a story." And this is what he told me as he sat in his car:

**TONY'S STORY:** My son is 21. He would be in his room for hours at a time, on Facebook. When people upset him online, he would storm through the house slamming doors. He's now left home. Then my three daughters—aged 16, 14 and 12—started spending every spare minute on Facebook. More of the same.

Finally, a month ago, I said to my girls, "Enough! You've got until Sunday night—then no more Facebook in this house!"

It's amazing! I can't believe the change. We talk to each other! My middle girl is getting fit. She goes jogging, she takes walks in the park. My little one is doing twice as much homework.

They are happier. We do things together. Their school results have improved. I have my family back!

Teenagers don't always know when too much is too much. Social networking can be great fun and a wonderful way to stay in touch. But when it stops being wonderful, parents need to take action.

**In a Nutshell**
Teenagers can survive—and thrive—without social networking.

## Signs That Your Child is Being Bullied at School

You say, "So what are the signs Mary is being bullied?" You might notice:

- She suddenly doesn't want to go to school. She manufactures all kinds of excuses not to go, she says she's sick but shows no symptoms.
- Mary has regular headaches, stomach aches and nausea ... the stress of being bullied will make your child sick.
- She doesn't sleep.
- Mary arrives home with injuries but no convincing explanations. For example, she has scratches on her neck and claims that she accidentally stepped on the neighbour's cat.
- She arrives home with torn clothing—or without items of clothing. Mary will decide it is better to "lose" a sweater than to bring it home, torn in half.
- She starts talking angrily about her classmates.
- Mary loses interest in spending time with friends—and doesn't even want to talk about them.

- Mary refuses to talk about anything concerned with school. Most kids will share stories about funny, silly, crazy things their friends do—except when they feel totally isolated and alone and there are no stories to share.
- Her school grades take a dive. (How can you perform at school when you are being threatened?)
- Mary starts going to school at strange times or via strange routes. That's one way to avoid the bullies.
- She begs you to drive her to school.
- She has no appetite.
- She is always hungry after school. If the bullies are stripping her of her lunch money, she'll be ravenous by the time she gets home.
- She seems permanently angry, upset, depressed. (Sure, some teens who aren't being bullied also display these symptoms.)

MATTHEWS

## Signs That Your Child is Being Cyber-Bullied

If Mary is being bullied at school, the bullies may also be harassing her in cyberspace.

If you notice she:

- suddenly starts spending much less time on the computer
- becomes noticeably more angry, depressed or withdrawn after using the computer
- looks uncomfortable whenever she receives emails or texts
- stops answering her phone or viewing texts in front of you
- won't discuss what she is doing on her computer, it is likely she is being cyber-bullied.

And don't be fooled. Some children who are being cyber-bullied spend *more time* on their laptop.

**Survival in Cyberspace:**

This is critical information for your child!

- You never know what will happen to messages or photos that you post or send. A trusted friend today may not be your friend tomorrow! So here's a test: IF YOU WOULDN'T WANT THE PHOTO OR MESSAGE SHARED WITH YOUR WHOLE SCHOOL—AND YOUR PARENTS—DON'T SEND IT.
- Never send photos or videos of yourself to people you have never met in real life.
- If someone is abusing you, you don't have to reply. Most people will give up if you ignore them. But keep records and report them.
- Most instant messaging software, chat sites and phones enable you to block people you don't want to hear from.
- If you wouldn't say something to someone's face, don't say it online. Anything that is nasty face-to-face, is nasty in cyberspace.
- Anything that is a crime in the real world is a crime in cyberspace.

The following websites have useful information on cyber-security:

- www.cyberangels.org
- www.kidscape.org.uk

Many educational websites provide interactive cyber-safety games for younger children—you can find these by doing a quick web search.

## Through the Eyes of a Teenager

It is easy for an adult to decide that a child—or a teen—should report a bully. But children don't have the wisdom or confidence of a grown-up.

Matthew recalls being bullied as a child: *"Most of what happened to me could have been prevented if I had reported it. But I didn't know any better. I didn't know what was considered*

> 66 *Most of what happened to me could have been prevented if I had reported it.* 99

*'average everyday' stuff versus something is 'definitely wrong here' stuff. I knew him a long time before all this started. I trusted him. So I didn't have any reason to believe he was doing me wrong."*

People sometimes talk of teens as having only fifteen or seventeen years experience in the world—*but they haven't even had that!*

A child spends his first eight or ten years learning the basics: learning to walk, feed himself, dress himself, learning the alphabet, learning about bicycles —but what does he know about relationships and resolving conflicts before he is ten? Nothing.

How many major problems does he solve before he is ten? Zero!

A fifteen-year-old hasn't had fifteen years experience in the real world. So:

- When he fails a subject, he thinks it is the end of the world.
- When he applies for a part-time job—and misses out, he is devastated—because it has never happened before.
- When his girlfriend dumps him, he wants to die. He has never survived a broken heart before—and he is not sure that he can.
- When some kid threatens to kill him, he thinks he might die!

## Mr Saunders

I had an English teacher in high school called Mr Saunders. He was over sixty. He was charismatic, intimidating and sarcastic. He was educated and entertaining—he quoted Wordsworth and Blake. He was my favourite teacher.

My parents knew him vaguely but they didn't like him. Mum said he was arrogant and conceited.

One night when I was fifteen, Mr Saunders came to our house. He had never come to our house before.

He sat with my parents in the lounge room, drinking port wine and making awkward conversation. I was writing an Asian history essay in my bedroom when, to my surprise, Mr Saunders appeared. It felt weird—like having the Prime Minister in your bedroom!

We chatted about my history homework. Suddenly, as if he was a doctor, he said, "Lift up your shirt, boy." I could only assume that Mr Saunders had some kind of medical background and that he suspected I had some disease. I lifted my shirt.

Then he said, "Drop your trousers!"

Drop your trousers? I thought, "This must be serious!" What do you do when the Prime Minister says, "Drop your trousers!"? I dropped my pants and he began to touch me. I expected him to say something like, "You've got a nasty case of Bacterius Upyouranus—you need antibiotics!" But he said nothing. He returned to the lounge room.

Twenty minutes later he was back and this time he told me to remove my clothes and lie on my bed. Mr Saunders sat beside me and the examination continued. Again he touched my genitals.

I thought, "It can't be syphillis! I'm a virgin!"

He said, "I'm going to touch you all over. Tell me what thoughts you have."

Nothing in my experience had prepared me for this. I had never even heard the word "paedophile" and I could not imagine that a sixty-year-old man would get pleasure from stroking my penis. I still didn't understand what was happening. My bedroom door was slightly ajar and I remember thinking: "Here I am lying naked with an old man. What if my parents walk by? How do I explain this?"

> **"I'm going to touch you all over. Tell me what thoughts you have."**

By now I realised that this was no medical examination. This was something very strange. I became more embarrassed and more confused! I couldn't believe that this teacher that I admired above all others—who had a wife and family— was some kind of sexual deviant.

I began to protest. Eventually Saunders gave up and left.

I was guilty of nothing but I told no one about Saunders. Though I knew my parents disliked him, I didn't tell them. Though I told my big brother my other secrets, I never told him. I hated to think about it and I hated Saunders. I had done nothing wrong but I was ashamed.

## "It's My Fault!"

How did I deal with it? I just wished Saunders was dead. I said to myself, "Hopefully he'll die soon and it will all be over." Even today it disturbs me. Even today I recall every detail. I write books about happiness and letting go of bad experiences—but the memory of that episode still makes my skin crawl.

Compared to millions of abused children, my experience at the hands of Mr

Saunders was minor. Here is the point of my story:

> Not once did I ask myself, "Should I tell my Mum and Dad?" THE IDEA THAT I MIGHT TELL MY PARENTS NEVER ENTERED MY HEAD. Never, ever, ever did I consider telling anyone.

Here's what my fifteen-year-old brain thought:
- you allowed your English teacher to fondle you
- there is no way that you can explain or justify that to anyone
- you are on your own, and
- you will suffer until the bastard drops dead.

It took me 30 years to talk about it.

A fifteen-year-old doesn't think like a logical adult. A fifteen-year-old thinks he is somehow to blame. A fifteen-year-old sees no way out. If an abused fifteen-year-old thinks like that, what hope is there for an eight-year-old?

When you are a child, and an adult does something that is NOT OKAY, you think: BECAUSE IT WAS AN ADULT THAT DID IT, IT MUST BE OKAY.

**In a Nutshell**
- Don't expect your teenager to think like an adult.
- Kids think that they are to blame even when they are not.

### "I Wanted to Live Longer But..."

*"Grandmother, please live a long life. Father, thank you for the trip to Australia. Mother, thank you for the delicious meals. I wanted to live longer, but . . ".*

So wrote Kiyoteru Okouchi from Aichi prefecture, Japan, before he tied a rope around his neck and hung himself from a tree. He was 13.

In his farewell note he described how over a period of three years, he had been tormented and tortured by four classmates. The bullies had extorted more than $10,000 from him—most of which he stole from his parents. The bullies beat him, they dunked his head in a river. They laughingly called him Number 1 Errand Boy.

During his final days, Okouchi's tormentors demanded another $400, but the young teen had no way to get it. In desperation Okouchi took his own life. Until he died he never told his parents. Even though his worried father asked him, "Are you being bullied? Are you taking money?" Okouchi never breathed a word.

The message to parents: if you suspect there is a problem, persist, persist. When it comes to bullying don't assume that your child will tell the truth. Many children don't.

> **66** *The bullies had extorted more than $10,000 from him.* **99**

**In a Nutshell**

No matter how deeply your child is in trouble, don't expect him to tell you about it.

## Brodie's Story

Brodie Panlock was a 19-year-old waitress at Cafe Vamp, in Victoria, Australia.

Three young men who also worked at the cafe set out to make her life a living hell. They called her "fat and ugly", they spat on her and they poured fish oil over her hair and clothes. They put rat poison in her bag and told her to take it. The humiliation continued six days a week for months.

In September 2006, when Brodie could take no more of the relentless abuse, she leapt to her death from a multi-story building.

The court case that followed grabbed worldwide attention. The judge described the offenders' behaviour as "vicious and persistent" as he convicted the three employees and fined them a total of $85,000. The owner of the cafe was also found guilty, and he and his company were fined a quarter of a million dollars for failing to provide a safe workplace.

Outside the court Brodie's mother Rae spoke of her daughter, "She was my little ray of sunshine, a very pretty girl... it just breaks your heart. As far as I'm concerned, they drove her to the edge and pushed her over... they should be in jail."

As of May 2011, workplace bullies in Victoria can be jailed.

Brodie's parents campaigned for justice for two years. Because of their efforts, and because of the community outrage over Brodie's bullying, the state Crimes Act was changed. In an amendment known as "Brodie's Law", the crime of stalking now includes "abusive words or acts" in the workplace. Workplace bullies in Victoria can now be found guilty of causing psychological harm and even causing suicide, and may serve up to ten years in prison.

In what is a familiar pattern:

- Brodie's parents knew nothing of the bullying. Here was a young woman—no longer at school—who chose suicide over quitting her job or telling her parents.

- Bystanders did nothing. Some of Brodie's friends knew of the bullying but none spoke to her parents or any authorities. Several customers knew of the bullying, but did nothing. What if one bystander had taken action?

## Listening when your Child is Bullied

Your twelve-year-old is being taunted at school. She is one of those rare children—the one in ten—who has decided to tell her parents. She comes to you traumatised and desperate.

What should you do?

First, listen! Before you start giving advice, ranting and raving or calling neighbours, just listen.

When your child is in trouble she needs to know that you care enough to give her your full attention. Turn off all distractions. Sit down somewhere quiet. Then:

- Get the whole story. If she is upset, just having the chance to tell you everything that happened—uninterrupted—will make her feel better.

- Let her know that you heard her and you understood. Repeat back to her what she said, "So you came around the corner and there was Mandy ... so you were scared..."

- Don't put words in her mouth, e.g. "Did she bully you?"

- Ask open-ended questions: "How did this start?" "What did he say?" What happened next?" Just listen.

- Thank her for telling you. Thank her for trusting you.

- Encourage her. You might say something like, "This has been very tough for you. You were very brave."

- Help her to feel that she can handle this. Help her to find solutions. "What could you have done?" "What would you say next time?"

It is so rare to be listened to. These days, how often do you try to chat with a sister, husband, lover—and they continue texting, playing Nintendo, watching

TV, fiddling with MySpace and taking phone calls? How important do you feel?

**In a Nutshell**

The greatest respect that you can pay anyone is to truly listen. The greatest comfort you can give a troubled child is to listen.

## Interfering

You have a son, Jim. One day Jim comes home from school crying, "Greg pushed me off my bike. He kicked me in the shins and smashed my transformer... " You feel steam coming from your ears. You want to call Greg's mother right now and tell her, "Your son is a bully. You make him leave my boy alone!"

Perfectly understandable reaction but not such a good idea.

Put yourself in Greg's mother's shoes. She knows nothing of this. She is in the middle of a supermarket and she just had an argument with her ex-husband. She gets your call telling her that her son is a bad kid.

If Greg's mother is like ninety percent of mothers, her reaction will be, "My son is not a bully. Your boy is a wimp."

So what should you do?

- Cool down. Fixing delicate issues when you are angry never works.
- Get the whole story from Jim. Things aren't always what they seem.
- Wait a few days. If your son isn't in serious danger, wait and see. Maybe it was an isolated incident.
- Remember that when you fix Jim's problems for him, you give Jim two messages: 1) "You are not able to fix this on your own", and 2) "Whenever you have a problem, I'll fix it". Neither of these messages is helpful.

If this boy, Greg, continues to bully your son, you may choose to speak to his parents. But take a different approach. For example, when you are feeling more relaxed, you might call Greg's mother and say, "Some of the boys in the school have been fighting. A group of parents are meeting for coffee..."

If you proceed with the meeting, avoid singling out one child. Keep it in the spirit of a group of concerned parents.

## Anti-Bullying Programs in Schools

Is this typical? The principal calls a school assembly to tackle bullying and a thousand kids gather in the gymnasium. A teacher gives a boring speech about why bullying is bad and announces the school's new zero tolerance bullying program. Throughout the presentation:

- **the bullies** pay no attention. They make jokes, pinch the kids in front of them and build paper aeroplanes,
- **the bullied kids** stare blankly into space. They are already so used to being punched, ridiculed and excluded that they believe they deserve it—and expect nothing will change, and
- **the silent majority**—the bystanders—learn no new skills to reduce bullying in the school.

Later that week, a teacher posts a sign in the hallway that says Zero Tolerance for Bullying. The school now has a new slogan to post on its website.

With all the extra attention, bullying INCREASES.

## Everyone Lives Life the Best Way They Know How

If you follow obese people into greasy hamburger joints and tell them, "You should eat bean sprouts", will they quit eating junk? If you tell a heavy smoker, "You should quit smoking!", will he quit? No!

Telling people how to live doesn't work. When you tell heavy smokers or heavy eaters to do it less, they do it more! It is no different for people who bully.

People do what they do for serious, deep-seated reasons. You telling them to stop makes no difference.

## So When Do They Stop?

Alcoholics quit drinking when they finally believe that life can be better without being drunk. The same principle applies for smokers—and bullies.

Some people believe that bullies will stop if you just tell them how the victim feels. Usually not says Katherine Newman in her book *Rampage: The Social Roots of School Shootings:* "The desire to behave better is a weak motivator compared to the status that comes from teasing and harassment..."

Begging bullies to be nice doesn't work. Punishing bullies usually doesn't stop them.

ANDREW MATTHEWS

Most bullies bully in public—to impress their peers, to look powerful. But when their peers are no longer impressed, there is no pay-off for the bully. When bystanders make it clear that bullying is unacceptable, things begin to change.

Stan Davis is an American counsellor, child and family therapist and founder of the International Bullying Prevention Association. He has focused on bullying prevention in schools since the late 1990's.

To summarise some of Davis' findings on school bullying:

- TELLING YOUTH WHO BULLY TO STOP DOESN'T WORK. They don't want to be told that they are bad people and they don't care enough to quit.
- TARGETS OF BULLYING OFTEN BELIEVE THAT THEY DESERVE IT and they already believe that they are doing something wrong. Telling the targets of bullying to behave differently reinforces their belief that they are to blame.
- ADVISING YOUNG PEOPLE TO CONFRONT BULLIES IS UNREALISTIC AND INEFFECTIVE. Expecting bystanders to risk their safety is neither reasonable nor intelligent.
- THE MAJORITY OF YOUNG PEOPLE ARE KIND AND SYMPATHETIC. It is easier to inspire a bystander to be kind than it is to change the behaviour of a bullying person.

This leaves us with just two groups who are strong enough and interested enough to change the school culture—the teachers and the bystanders. Says Davis, "I've come to work primarily with staff and bystanders because these two groups define what behaviours are acceptable and unacceptable".

# Bullying at Home

## 3

## Gordon's Story

Until I was eleven, my biggest fear was that my father would leave home. After eleven, my biggest fear was that he would come back. Dad first left us when I was ten—and like most kids, I thought it was my fault.

He returned home when I was eleven. I was happy, anxious, hopeful, scared—would he love us enough to stay? Would we become a normal family and play football in the park, would we go on vacation like normal kids?

My excitement was short-lived. Within two weeks Dad called me aside. I was the youngest child—God knows why he chose to tell me and no one else—he just said, "I can't stay here. I don't love your mother and I don't love you kids". And he walked out.

> **Dad first left us when I was ten—and like most kids, I thought it was my fault.**

I was gutted. "What is the matter with me? What is the matter with us?"

It was another two years before we saw him again. Suddenly, in 1974, he showed up for Christmas lunch. I was thrilled—we were going to have a normal family celebration!

Mum decorated the table and made a special effort. But Dad was unhappy with the entree and went crazy: "What the F***! My maintenance money is going towards prawn cocktails!"

With that, he jumped to his feet, grabbed the dining table and with one almighty heave, he hurled it toward my mother. The impact of the table top hitting Mum's forehead bounced her against the wall. She went down in a shower of plates, glasses and Christmas decorations. Poor Mum was unconscious before she hit the floor. Dad had been home for just twenty minutes.

He stormed out—and never came home again.

## The Silent Treatment

Dad hated Mum, so he punished her by humiliating his kids. He would call us

*Stupid* or *Idiot*. For as long as I remember, I never had a conversation with him.

I was a good soccer player—which should have been a joy—except that Dad made it hell. Before a game he would promise me 20 cents if I scored a goal. If I didn't score a goal, he wouldn't talk to me for three days.

He punished me by not speaking to me. It happened over and over. I suffered more from Dad's silent treatment than from any of his verbal bullying. I thought, "You bastard!"

Parents don't realise that the silent treatment can hurt far more than physical beatings.

I shared a bedroom with my older brother, David. Because Dad was a bully, David was a bully. David beat me almost daily. I would hide under the covers, pretending I was asleep but it didn't help.

Mostly, David hit me for no reason—but when he had a reason, he was brutal. Eight years older than me, David had a pair of really cool moccasins. One day when I was twelve and David was at work, I borrowed them. I felt so proud and so grown-up. I walked to the shopping mall feeling like Elvis! When I got back I carefully returned the shoes to exactly the same spot in his wardrobe, just where I had found them. But I forgot to untie the laces.

David came home and found out I had worn his shoes. I was sitting in the lounge room when David approached me from behind. With one huge punch to my head, he launched me into space. I landed beside the television, unconscious.

I woke up to find my mother outstretched on the floor nearby, with my brother and sister crouched over her. She had witnessed David's vicious attack and fainted.

Andrew Matthews

## Constant Fear

After the Christmas celebration, Mum was hospitalised with a total nervous breakdown. She lost herself in a haze of alcohol and tablets for several years and I was more or less on my own. For me, being lonely and being scared was just normal.

Funny isn't it? Most kids dread having their parents look at their school reports. I just wished that someone, anyone would care enough to look at mine!

I lived in constant fear. I feared that Mum would die of an overdose—or that she would drive off a cliff. I feared going to school—I had no confidence, I couldn't make friends and I was a bad student. I was scared to come home because I knew what was waiting for me—a beating from my brother.

There was this song I knew. I would play it in my head over and over to give me courage:

*Walk tall, walk straight and look the world right in the eye*
*That's what my mama told me when I was about knee high.*
*Walk tall, walk straight...*[3]

I sang it every day. The song gave me strength.

Sometimes there is just one person in your life who gives you some hope. In my case, there was a teacher, Mr Pearsal, who knew about my problems at home. Mr Pearsal made a special effort to talk to me at school. He gave me one-on-one time, and that made me feel really special. Sometimes he would collect me from my house and take me to the local swimming pool. He will never know how much it meant to me—to have one adult treating me with kindness.

## Who Could Love Me?

Because Dad left us when I was young, I expected other people to abandon me. I couldn't believe that anyone could love me, and that made me insanely jealous. I divorced twice before I was thirty. I was so scared that my wives would walk out, I found excuses to leave them before they left me first.

I am now fifty and I still hurt. But gradually I have come to accept that I am a nice person. I have compassion. I have had a beautiful partner, Natalie, for

> 66 With one huge punch to my head, he launched me into space. I landed beside the television, unconscious. 99

> 66 Sometimes there is just one person in your life who gives you some hope. 99

41

ten years, and we have four children we love dearly. We are kind to each other.

For the last twenty years I have owned restaurants. I can deal with angry customers because I understand that they are not really angry at me. They are simply angry people. I don't take it personally. You can choose how much you let them affect you—or upset you. Why should you let people you don't like or respect, ruin your day? It is not what is happening to you, it is what you perceive is happening.

Respecting people and respecting their feelings is an important thing in my life.

## Forgiveness

Because my father bullied my mother and us kids, because my mum whipped me with a dog lead and my brother beat me up, I swore that I would never bully another human being. I promised myself that I would never hurt someone emotionally like my father hurt me.

> **" I worked hard to forgive my father—for my sake. "**

When I was in my late twenties I met some kind people and I got some help. I read some self-help books. I managed to change my life around. I had had years of resentment, anger, sadness, jealousy and hurt. It controlled my life and damn near ruined my life.

I worked hard to forgive my father—for my sake.

Although we each live a long way apart, I see my father, mother and my brother when I can. As I learned to forgive them my life became a whole lot better.

I never imagined that one day I would have a normal life and a family. For the first time I have a sense of stability. My children have given me meaning, and a reason to grow up, a reason to stop being the wounded little boy.

Today I counsel and coach teenagers. What do I tell them?

- No one can make you inferior without your consent.
- You can break the bullying cycle.

Gordon's email: gke13182@bigpond.net.au

# Why Bullies Bully

## 4

## Richard Plotkin

Fifty-nine-year-old Richard Plotkin lived alone in a cottage in the seaside town of Rosebud, Victoria. A loner and a little eccentric, he was well-known to the Rosebud locals who knew him as Smokey because he smoked a lot.

Richard was born into an educated family—his father was a successful solicitor and member of parliament. Richard was a bright child. He played musical instruments, excelled at writing and won prizes for his poetry.

He would be seen around town in his sheepskin jacket and long beard. He drank coffee at his favourite cafe and ate at Vinnie's Kitchen. Vinnie's Kitchen is a place where volunteers serve meals to those in need. He would walk the streets at night but he worried nobody. He hurt no one.

Richard was an easy target for a group of five local bullies—aged 18 to 20—who taunted him "just for fun". One time, they tried to set fire to his beard with a cigarette lighter. Another time outside the Rosebud Hotel, they threw a tub of cream over his head. Their friend—a young girl—filmed the attack and uploaded it to YouTube.

> **" One time, they tried to set fire to his beard with a cigarette lighter. "**

Sergeant Scott Barnes said later, "These guys seemed to have a bee in their bonnet about Richard."

Barnes explained, "On September 30, 2008 the five young men were bored and looking for something to do. One suggested that they should go to Smokey's house and set fire to his front door.

"So around midnight, armed with a plastic watering can half full of petrol, they arrived at Richard's home. Pretending to be police, they knocked on the door and called out, 'Richard, it's Constable Smitty from the Rosebud Police Station'. When Richard came to the door, they threw the petrol. It splashed onto the door and onto his head and chest."

It took several attempts to start the fire. Finally two of the men used petrol residue in the can to create a Molotov-like cocktail—and then threw the burning can at a front window. The burning can smashed through the glass and Richard and his house went up in flames.

The five men sped away.

With his clothes and flesh on fire, Richard escaped by throwing himself through the same front window. Neighbours later found him beside the road. Richard was unrecognisable—dazed, horrifically burned and confused as to why the "police" would set him alight.

When detectives later visited the scene they found the charred patch of ground where Richard was discovered. His clothes were reduced to ash save a few fragments.

Richard's home was totally destroyed.

## Richard's Injuries

Richard suffered fourth-degree burns to more than half of his body. He had no ears, no lips, no eyelids left.

An air ambulance rushed him to Alfred Hospital in Melbourne where doctors induced him into a coma. Richard spent weeks in intensive care fighting for his life. He received skin grafts to his back, neck, shoulders, scalp and fingers.

The Victorian Arson and Explosives Squad went to work on the case. They door-knocked Rosebud and appealed for witnesses. They interviewed friends of the bullies and viewed CCTV footage. Forensic chemists scoured the crime scene.

Sergeant Barnes recalls, "Locals reported that the boys were skylarking about how they had burnt Richard. There were some messages on MySpace where one of the boys talked about setting fire to a house."

Within nine days all five offenders were arrested.

Initially, all five denied any involvement. One by one, as they realised the ringleader of the group was in custody and admitted he was guilty, they changed their story. The ringleader was particularly cocky. On his arrest he asked police, "Is there a gym at the police station I can use?"

When all five men admitted to their part in the crime, none considered their offence to be particularly serious. One explained, "We were talking about having a laugh and getting up to a bit of mischief... ".

Richard will be grossly disfigured for the rest of his life. He will require rehabilitation and ongoing surgery for the rest of his life. How does one describe this crime... stupid, callous, unnecessary, bullying gone mad? It's a tragedy for a harmless man whose life will never be the same. It's a tragedy for five families.

When the case went to court, veteran court reporters said that they had never before seen such public interest in a case.

At the court hearing, the magistrate Peter Couzens demanded to hear from the parents. One mother offered to help Richard in hospital, "... if I could feed him, if I could put his eye drops in and help him through for the rest of his life..." Another mother said she could not believe that her "good boy" had been involved.

> **Which mother imagines that her beautiful three-year-old son will one day grow up to set helpless people on fire?**

Five lives were destroyed. The lives of five families were ruined. Which mother imagines that her beautiful three-year-old son will one day grow up to set helpless people on fire?

Three of the group had prior involvements with police—but the other two had no prior involvements.

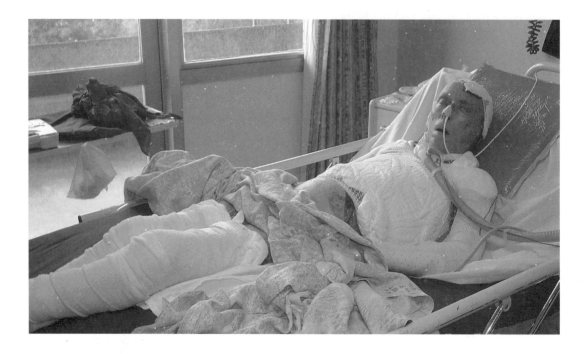

## No Innocent Bystanders

Something happens when people get together.

When a bunch of people set out to help—let's say a community sets out to build a school or a hospital or raise money for a sick child—they can work miracles. A group achieves more than one person might ever imagine.

But when a bunch of people set out to hurt, they do more damage than one person might ever imagine.

Only one man had the idea to light a fire. Only one man threw the petrol. Only one man threw the burning container. All five are in jail.

> **There is no such thing as an innocent bystander.**

The police prosecution argued that all five were responsible—and the judge agreed. The message from the court was, "There is no such thing as an innocent bystander." The message to each bully was:

- You chose to be there.
- At any time you could have said, "This is not right!"
- You drove away from a man who was on fire.
- You never called the fire brigade or ambulance.
- You never contacted police.
- You knew it was a crime but you did it.

Where were the bystanders?

The young girl who recorded the cream attack for YouTube knew it was wrong to bully an innocent man. She knew it was wrong to record it.

At any stage she could have:
- refused to record the video
- deleted the video
- told the boys, "You're a bunch of cowards! Leave this man alone."
- told her parents, or
- told the police.

She did nothing. What if she had spoken out?

After the fire, several witnesses to previous bullying attacks on Richard contacted police. These witnesses could have helped Richard while there was still time. They could have told the bullies to stop bullying a defenceless man, they could have telephoned the police and perhaps averted the tragedy. But no one did anything.

## The Outcome

Sergeant Scott Barnes reflects, "The successful outcome of this investigation can be attributed to the assistance and public outcry from the Greater Mornington Peninsula community who were deeply affected by this senseless act—and to the exceptional work by all areas of Victoria Police that were involved including; Homicide Squad, Surveillance Unit, Regional Tasking Units and the entire office at the Arson and Explosives Squad."

The court appointed Victoria's Office of the Public Advocate as his guardian. The Office of the Public Advocate uphold the rights and interests of people with a disability and work to eliminate abuse, neglect and exploitation.

Staff from the Office of the Public Advocate were committed to ensuring justice for Richard Plotkin. His legal guardian Leon O'Brien, prepared a powerful Victim Impact Statement for the court on his behalf. Media adviser Sally Gibson ensured that the media coverage respected his privacy as much as possible while also highlighting the horrific nature of the case.

Says Sally Gibson, "Leon was an absolute hero during the case and continues to be."

Today Richard Plotkin is totally destroyed.

**In a Nutshell**

If you are a bystander to bullying—and you do nothing—you are part of the problem.

### The Wrong Crowd

What do most parents say when their children get into serious trouble? "He got in with the wrong crowd!" It's the typical knee-jerk reaction: parents blame THE FRIENDS.

If your daughter got in with the wrong crowd, here are the first questions you need to ask:

- If it is the wrong crowd, why does she like them?
- If it is the wrong crowd, why do they like her?
- What is it about the wrong crowd that feels good?

And the big question: IF SHE IS IN BAD COMPANY, WHAT HAVE YOU DONE TO GET HER OUT?

### Is Your Child a Bully?

Want to upset your neighbours in a hurry? Try telling them any of the following:

- "You're ugly"
- "You're stupid"
- "You're a loser", or if you really want to upset them
- "Your child is a bully!"

When you confront the parents of bullies they become angry and defensive. They say things like:

- he was just teasing
- he's not a bully, he is just confident
- she's no bully, your girl is a wimp.

Bullies come in all shapes and sizes. Some are popular and some are outcasts. They can be strangers or family friends. Some bullies are Jekyll and Hyde characters—a friend one day and a torturer the next. Matthew describes the bully who terrorised him for three years:

> Yes, I knew the bully. He outweighed me by at least 70 pounds. He was a grade ahead of me, but two years older. I had looked up to him as a role model. I thought he was perfect. My parents and his parents were best friends. So we "ran into" each other a lot since the time I was in first grade. I can remember sitting in the far back of his parents' station wagon with him going places. I remember being in his house.
>
> Some said he was the strongest kid in school. He could play any sport. (I still hate sports.) He was in the band. He had a beautiful voice. The girls thought he was the cutest boy in the school. Why he needed attention from picking on me I'll never know.

So what are some clues that your child may be a bully? If your child:
- struggles to make friends
- has little concern for the feelings of other children
- often excludes certain children from playing games
- has witnessed regular verbal or physical violence at home, or
- suddenly arrives home with toys or clothes that you didn't buy him—or money that you didn't give him, you may have a bully on your hands.

## Girls versus Boys

When boys make fun of other boys, they usually question their sexuality. They label their targets as "gay", "faggot", "queer", "queen", "poofta".

When girls bully other girls, they mostly criticize their morals. So they use words like "slut", "whore", "hooker", "tart" and "bitch".

Boys have always punched and wrestled—but punching, wrestling and kicking is becoming more common amongst girls.

Girls in particular have taken to cyber-bullying because:
- girls are less confrontational—cyber-bullying can be done from a distance

- girls are better equipped to engage in psychological and emotional bullying, and

- girls, as a whole, have superior verbal skills.

### Two Kinds of Bullies

Research by Norwegian Professor Dan Olweus and others confirms what you already know—there are two basic groups of bullies:

**Bullied Bullies:** are bullied at home or at school or both. They have few friends and low status amongst their peers. They are lonely and disconnected.

Bullied bullies are the children usually responsible for school massacres—they are the kids who couldn't take it anymore. As Eric Harris, one of the Columbine shooters, said, "This is what you get for the way you treated us".

**"Cool" Bullies:** are the more typical bullies. Cool bullies appear confident and they have high status.

Professor Olweus began studying bullying in the 1970s—and he is one of the founding fathers of bullying research. Summarising his own findings on typical bullies and self-esteem he said:

*"There was nothing in the results to support the common view (that bullies suffer from low self-esteem)... The bullies had unusually little anxiety and insecurity... They did not suffer from poor self-esteem."* [4]

A 2003 study of 1,985 sixth-graders reached the same conclusion: that bullies were less likely than non-bullies to show signs of depression, anxiety or loneliness. It also showed that bullies were more popular amongst their peers than non-bullies. [5]

All the bullying research shows that some popular children are bullies. But many popular kids never hurt anybody. So how do we explain that? Here's what most bullying books and websites don't make clear: according to psychologists, there are two very different kinds of popular children:

- WELL-LIKED popular: these children are regarded as trusted, kind, thoughtful and friendly, and

- PERCEIVED popular: these children are socially prominent, and are envied or admired. Other students may see them as strong, sporty, talented, beautiful, influential—but not necessarily nice!  Their classmates may label them as "arrogant" or "stuck-up".

The cool bullies come from this second group—perceived as being popular. They taunt, ridicule, bully and exclude to maintain their social position.

Both bullied bullies and cool bullies have little empathy for their victims.

**In a Nutshell**
Bullied bullies have had too much pain to care how others feel—and cool bullies haven't had enough.

## "I Don't Try Anymore"

**TED'S STORY:** It's 7:40am. I'm exhausted and I have to leave for school in 15 minutes. I played Grand Theft Auto until 3am. The one time I don't hate myself—and my life—is when I'm playing video games.

I hate school. Everyone makes fun of me. Kids trip me up, they steal my sandwiches or spit on me and run away. Last week they broke my bike. I just try to avoid people.

I hate school because I have no friends and I'm stupid.

I can never remember names and dates. In examinations, my brain freezes. I can't explain it. I have always been the class dunce. Teachers ask me questions, I panic and answer wrong, everyone laughs.

Other kids cruise through school—they can write fancy sentences, they can do equations—and they get good grades without even trying. They think they are so smart.

I have tried making an effort, but even when I do my best, it's hopeless. Once I spent a whole weekend writing and rewriting a history essay. I was determined to score my first "A". I never worked so hard on anything. For a whole week I dreamed about arriving home from school with the news, "Mum, Dad, I got an "A". Then the teacher returned the marked essays.

I failed.

I cried for three hours. I punched a hole in my bedroom wall. I tried to talk to my dad about it. Dad had his own explanation. Dad just said: "You're stupid."

I don't try any more. It hurts too much to try.

Some other kids are a bit like me—not real smart—but they are football stars, or they are *beautiful* or *handsome*. I'm fat and sweaty.

I can't run, I can't catch a ball. I hate my fat ass, I hate my chubby, pimply face and my straight, greasy hair. I avoid mirrors. If I see my reflection in a shop window, I say to myself, "You fat, ugly bastard".

Some kids aren't smart, aren't sports stars and aren't beautiful—but they are witty. They have *personality*. Not me. I'm boring. Sometimes I try to be funny—other kids look at me like I'm weird. I'm starting to think I am weird.

> 66 *Dad just said: "You're stupid."* 99

My parents both work. They are always busy and they hardly talk. So at home I eat by myself. Dad is always angry. I know he's disappointed in me.

Dad used to beat me. He hit me when I broke things or forgot stuff. And when Dad got drunk, which was most days, he hit me for nothing. Now I'm too big to hit—so now Dad just hits Mum. I feel sorry for my Mum. She's got her own problems.

Mum calls me "Teddy" and Dad calls me "Stupid"... "Hey Stupid, get your ass in here!" At school they don't call me Stupid. At school they call me *Blubber*, *Porker*, *Fatso*, *Earthquake*—but anything is better than your dad calling you *Stupid*.

I walk to school—alone. I walk like I'm real confident, like I'm this tough guy who doesn't care. But you know what? Inside, I'm crying—all day, every day. I wish I had just one friend—one friend who didn't think I was a retard.

Sometimes, on the way to school, I come across Jamie. Jamie is younger than me and real small. Jamie has a smart mouth.

I smack him around... I'll tell him, "I'll teach you a lesson you little faggot". Sure, I'll twist his arm or rub his face in the mud. Yesterday I took his lunch money. Is it bullying? Everybody does it.

So here is Ted the bully who grew up being bullied. Ted hates himself. He is ashamed of himself. He bullies Jamie to try to forget that his own life is a living hell.

> 66 *I wish I had just one friend—one friend who didn't think I was a retard.* 99

QUESTION: If Dad steps in and says, "You are a bully and a loser. Shame on you. I'm confiscating your computer." Would that help?

QUESTION: If Jamie's mum corners Ted in the street and shouts, "You are a loser and a fat prick." Would that help?

QUESTION: If the school principal says, "Shame on you!

You are suspended for a week!" Would that solve the problem?

QUESTION: How much do you need to punish Ted until he becomes a normal, happy kid?

No kid deserves to suffer like Ted.

## What do Bullies Want?

Bullies want what anybody else wants.

Bullies want:

- to feel loved by their parents
- to be popular with their friends
- to be good at something, and
- to feel in control of their life.

Bullies want to feel clever, powerful, appreciated.

Everyone wants to be good at something—good at schoolwork, good at sport, even good at being a nice person, or good at being a good son or daughter, good at feeling good about themselves.

But when a kid feels unloved, disliked, incompetent—and if he has spent his life being smacked around and ridiculed—he may well adopt the strategy of so many delinquents:

*"If you don't like me,*
*at least you'll notice me!*
*If I can't be good at being good,*
*I'll be good at being bad!*
*I'll be good at smashing things and beating up people.*
*I'll be good at making you feel bad.*
*The worse you look, the better I look.*
*The worse you feel, the better I feel."*

And bullies have excuses like:

- because other kids do it
- because he deserves it
- because it's what the in-crowd does
- because it makes me feel superior, or
- so other kids won't bully me.

**Bullies Enjoy Power**

You've seen children who bully, for example:

- Six-year-old Tommy who is in the playground with his little sister. When Tommy thinks no one is watching, he grabs her ear and twists it. She is screaming but he doesn't let go. On Tommy's face is a look of relish ... "I'm powerful! She deserves it and I'm doing this because I can!"

- Four high school kids who single out a classmate because he is overweight. There's a group of them and they attack like a group of piranhas ..."Hey Blubberguts ... Fatso, when did you last see your feet? ... you're disgusting ... hey Loser."

They don't attack out of anger, they attack out of disgust, contempt. They have no respect.

Bullies don't pick on people because they are upset with them, they pick on people they regard as inferior. They look for a weak target and then find excuses for why that person deserves to be attacked, "She's ugly, she's fat, he's a cry-baby."

Bullies believe: *I'm better than you are. I can be as cruel as I want because you are worth nothing.*

**In a Nutshell**

Bullying is not about anger. Bullying is about power, bullying is about contempt.

# Girl Bullying

## 5

## What Girls Value

Peter and Mandy go on a date. Next day, Mandy gets together with her best friend, Tanya. The girls spend an hour and a half reviewing every detail. Tanya has a hundred questions: "How was it? What did you wear? What did he say? And what did you say? How does he kiss? Where did you go? Was he romantic? Is it love?"

Next day Peter meets his best buddy, Todd. Todd asks, "Did you score?"

With girls it's all about THE RELATIONSHIP. As one soccer coach noted: *"If I got a bunch of boys together who didn't know each other and sent them out to play soccer, they wouldn't think twice about it. They'd go out and play, then go off the field and never think about seeing each other again.*

*Not so with girls. They need to know who is the leader, who they might become friends with, who's nice, who's popular, all that stuff before they can play anything."* 6

There are exceptions, but mostly:

- for girls it's about connection and relationships. Even at four years old it's, "You are my best friend" and "Let's all skip rope together"
- for boys it's about independence and competition. Even at four years old it's, "I'm the king of the castle" and "My dad can beat up your dad".

The pattern continues into adulthood: take any group of men and women at any table at any restaurant. At some point a woman will say, "I'm going to the ladies room. Who wants to come?" With women it's a group thing, a chance to bond, chat.

But when did you last see a guy stand up and say, "I'm going to the toilet. Who wants to join me?" For men it's about independence! That's why men hate to ask for directions: "I can find the airport, hotel, hospital—and the toilet—by myself!"

Men tell jokes because that makes them impressive. Women tell secrets because that builds relationships.

For men, its activities that hold relationships together—so two guys can fish together all day and never speak. And two women can speak together all day and never fish.

**In a Nutshell**

Because it's relationships that matter most to girls, it's in relationships that girls hurt each other most.

### Girl Wars

Males are programmed to solve disagreements by belting each other. Animals do it—watch a pair of stallions fighting—or male giraffes, goats or gorillas. Watch kangaroos box! It's the testosterone, and its how the male brain works.

Also, boys have all the aggressive role models. You have seen those movies where two guys arrange to fight each other outside the schoolyard or the saloon. They thump each other until they can't stand up. Then, covered in dust, with bloodied noses and broken teeth, they leave as friends. It's over, forgotten.

With girls it's more complex. Girls use rumour and exclusion—psychologists call it relational bullying. "Today you are my best friend, tomorrow you are history." Schoolgirls' friendships are more intense, like love affairs. The hurt runs deeper and lasts longer.

### "I Felt Like I Had Been Stabbed!"

**JANE'S STORY:** Alana was my best friend. She was long-limbed and elegant with thick, dark curls. I was plain and stumpy. I felt so privileged to be her friend. I loved her more than life itself. We spent our days together and our evenings talking on the phone. I dressed to please her and I tried to impress her with my wit. Then one day she called me and said, "It's over."

Alana had new friends. I felt like I had been stabbed. I curled up into a ball and cried for hours. My mother rocked me as I sobbed.

Alana and her new group had agreed that I was a loser. "Don't hang out with Jane. You might end up looking like her!" and "Hey, Jane. Did you take your ugly pills?"

The taunting continued for three years. I would find graffiti scrawled on my locker in thick black marker, "Dumb bitch". It was a campaign to destroy me and I didn't know why. Still don't know why. All I knew was that I was ugly and that there was something wrong with me. I was crushed. I tried to make new friends but I was damaged. I became depressed. I was so stressed, I pulled out all my eyelashes. I began to fail classes.

It took me six years to recover—but then I am not sure that I ever really recovered.

> **❝ I would find graffiti scrawled on my locker in thick black marker, 'Dumb bitch'. ❞**

## "Overnight I Was an Outcast"

**ELLIE'S STORY:** There was a group of us: the "cool kids". We were all on the basketball team. We all lived in the same part of town. Then one day my best friend Sharon asked me to a "meeting" in the hallway. There were seven girls there: Sharon announced, "You are not our friend anymore. You aren't cool enough." Another girl said, "Yeah, you are an embarrassment". And that was it.

I tried to talk to them. I was ignored. I would offer to share my lunch with them but they would all move away—like I had some disease.

Overnight I became an outcast, shunned in the schoolyard and excluded from all birthday parties, all sleepovers.

And there were the rumours. I was fifteen, an innocent virgin. They would hand me notes in class, "Lesbian slut. Whore". What can you do when the whole class is laughing at you? I became a loner. I avoided people, avoided any eye contact. I spent my last three years of high school just trying to be invisible.

What gives people the right to ruin another person's life?

If you are a woman, you know about all this. It is a big surprise to most guys—boyfriends, husbands and fathers—to learn that with girls, there is so much going on below the surface.

### Girl Secrets

Michelle Mitchell, author of *What Girls Don't Tell Their Parents* says that with girls "what you see is not what you get. Teens have a cover and an inside story."

She says, "What's happening inside and outside are two different things. Teens don't really hate their parents! When I ask teenage girls would you trust you?" they say to me, "What are you an idiot? Of course I wouldn't trust me!"

"So they know they need protecting. Teens want protection. Teens don't want to look like they can't handle their lives so they keep toxic friendships hidden."

She advises parents, "Help your teenager have control of the communication process. Kids come home and they get a barrage of questions but teenagers don't work like that. Tell them, 'I'm here whenever you want to talk about this—and you'll be surprised how often they will come and talk to you!"

## 6

# Tips for Bullied Kids

### "Everyone Gets Teased!"

Parents and teachers sometimes say, "Teasing is normal." Teasing IS normal. But teasing is not bullying. There is a big difference: Teasing is what happens amongst real friends.

EXAMPLE: John and his buddies are having lunch—John is famous for his big appetite. After he has demolished three hamburgers and two apple pies, his friend Nick turns to him and says, "Not hungry?" Everybody laughs, including John.

EXAMPLE: Karen and her friends are all around seventeen years old. Karen's ten year old neighbour, Jimmy, has a crush on her—the little guy is totally lovestruck. Karen is complaining that she doesn't have a boyfriend, to which her friends reply, "You've got Jimmy!" Everybody laughs, including Karen.

Healthy teasing happens among equals:

- teasing is innocent fun
- it is playful and well-meaning
- the teasing is a two-way thing
- when friends joke together, everybody laughs
- friends don't hurt your feelings on purpose. If one becomes upset, the teasing stops.

Taunting or verbal bullying happens when there is an imbalance of power:

- bullying is intended to harm. It is nasty, critical, intended to humiliate and embarrass
- it is a one-way thing
- the bully laughs but the target of the bullying doesn't

*"Just teasing!"*

- when the target becomes distressed, the taunting increases.

Some things are not right. Stealing is not right. People might say, "Everybody does it!" No they don't! It is the same with bullying.

## It's Not Your Fault

Some people like to smash things. They tear seats out of bus shelters, they throw rocks through windows, they set fire to people's mail boxes. They spot a shiny Porsche—and then they take a key and gouge the paintwork from end to end.

Do they scratch a beautiful Porsche because there is something wrong with it? NO! They attack it because there is something RIGHT with it.

- Vandals have no respect.
- Vandals just want to cause damage, somewhere!
- If there is no nice car to destroy, they smash something else.

BULLIES ARE THE SAME!

- Bullies have no respect.
- Bullies just want to cause damage, somewhere!
- If you weren't around, they would bully someone else.

Do you see? If you are being bullied, YOU ARE NOT THE PROBLEM. You are not being bullied because there is something wrong with you. Often, bullies attack you because there is something right with you. For example, a bully may not like it that:

- you are smart
- you are a computer wizard
- you come from a happy family
- you study hard
- you have more money than he has
- you look happier than she is
- you are a decent person!
- you have the courage to be different.

A bully may bully you because:

- he is bored
- he is selfish
- he is mean.

You have a right to feel safe and secure. If you are being bullied at school, it is the school's responsibility to stop it. If you are being harassed or attacked outside of school, the police have a responsibility to help you.

**In a Nutshell**
If you are being bullied, it doesn't mean there is something wrong with you. Did you get that?

IF YOU ARE BEING BULLIED, IT DOESN'T MEAN THERE IS SOMETHING WRONG WITH YOU.

## Tips to Deal With Bullies - What Works

Books and websites give bullied people lots of advice. You probably know that some strategies work better than others.

In 2010 the Youth Voice Research Project surveyed 13,000 students. The aim was to find out which strategies bullied kids found most helpful.

**HERE ARE THE STRATEGIES THAT MORE OFTEN HELPED, starting with number 1, the most helpful:**

1. TELL ONE OF YOUR PARENTS—OR ANY ADULT AT HOME. You say, "What can my parents do?" EVEN IF THEY DON'T DO ANYTHING, YOU WILL PROBABLY FEEL BETTER.

   When we tell someone about a problem, we understand the problem better—just by talking about it. Parents aren't perfect—but they usually care more than anyone else cares. They deserve to know and they want to know.

   Telling someone doesn't mean you are weak. In life you often need to get help from other people. When you have a broken leg, you get help from a doctor—it doesn't mean you are weak. If you are being bullied you need to ask for help.

2. TELL A FRIEND. Bullies want you to keep quiet. When you speak up, you refuse to play the bully's game. Telling others about the problem is a brave move. You don't have to do it alone.

3. TELL AN ADULT AT SCHOOL. It is the teacher's job to help you. If the first teacher doesn't help, tell another and another.

4. MAKE A JOKE ABOUT THE BULLYING. You might even agree with the bully. Bullies feel superior when you get upset or argue. Sometimes it helps to agree with them. Let's say you have skinny legs. You know you have skinny legs—you wish you didn't, but it's a fact. So the bully says:

   "Hey, your legs are like chopsticks."

   You, with a smile, "I know!"

   "Man, they are REALLY skinny!"

   "I know."

   The bully is hoping that you will take the bait and argue, burst into tears. Bully: "Hey four-eyes!"

You: "You don't like my glasses?"

Bully: "Right!"

You: "I don't like them either!"

5. REMIND YOURSELF THAT IT'S NOT YOUR FAULT

6. PRETEND IT DOESN'T BOTHER YOU—not easy, but some students—particularly older teenagers, found it useful.

7. LEAVE THE SCENE. Just because a bully starts an argument doesn't mean you have to hang around and finish it.

8. IGNORE THE BULLY. Pretend the teaser is invisible. Pretend to be deaf—or pretend that you are protected by an invisible shield—visualise all the insults just bouncing off.

**These are strategies that bullied kids found usually made the bullying WORSE:**

1. MAKING PLANS FOR REVENGE.

2. TELLING THE BULLY HOW YOU FEEL. Bullies want you to be upset and angry! The reason they bully is they don't care.

3. DOING NOTHING.

4. TELLING THE BULLY TO STOP. Lots of books and websites will tell you to tell the bully to stop. But bullies want a reaction—plenty of bullied children found that the more you tell a bully to stop, the more he will bully.

And finally, the strategy that is most likely to make the bullying worse:

5. HITTING THE BULLY. This works in movies. In real life it is most likely to backfire.

When you are cornered by bullies, you must make a stand—but that doesn't mean you hit them! It makes no sense to thump someone—or a whole group—who are bigger than you.

Your safety is most important. If the bully decides to steal your money or your stuff, let it go. Material things can be replaced.

## Some General Advice

Nobody deserves to be bullied. No matter how you walk or talk—no matter what you wear—nobody has the right to attack you.

You shouldn't have to change your behaviour to suit a bully.

ANDREW MATTHEWS

Still, there are some simple things to remember that can help in all relationships, including where bullies are concerned:

## Stay Cool

Sometimes people will say things to test you. They might tell you things like:

- "you're fat!"
- "you're ugly!"
- "your team sucks!"
- "your boyfriend is a nerd!"

As strange as it may seem, you don't have to get angry. You have a choice—you're not a robot.

There are many reasons why bullies bully:

- they want to feel tough
- they want to feel better than you
- they want entertainment.

Most often, they are just testing you to see how you will react. They want to see if they can make you angry. If you get angry, they win!

If you don't give them what they want, they will leave you alone.

Bullies want to get into a conversation. They want to show off to an audience. This is the kind of conversation they want:

Bully: You're fat.

Target: I am not.

Bully: Look at you—you're a whale!

Target: I'm not a whale.

Bully: Okay—you're a walrus!

Target: Why are you picking on me?

Bully: Because you're fat—and you stink.

Target: I do not.

Bully: And you are retarded. Just like your sister!

Target: Leave my sister out of it—

Bully: And that stupid haircut of yours...

## You Don't Have to Argue

While you continue to answer them, they keep abusing you. So don't play their game. This is the kind of conversation they don't want—because it is boring:

Bully: You're fat.

Target: Maybe.

Bully: You're so fat you could sink a ship.

Target: Maybe.

Bully: You're ugly.

Target: Maybe.

Bully: And you are stupid.

Target: Maybe.

Bully: You stink.

Target: Maybe.

Bully: Is that all you can say?

Target: Maybe.

Bully: All he says is "Maybe!"

Target: Maybe.

Bullies want a conversation. Don't give it to them. When you speak, keep it brief. Maximum, four or five words—and repeat yourself over and over. If the bully gets no reaction, he will often go away.

If you can avoid the bullies, AVOID them. If you know where the bullies are, go somewhere else! Stay away from them.

Some people say, "I refuse to run away—I refuse to look like a chicken!" Look at it this way. If a wild tiger escaped in your neighbourhood, would you be wandering around outside in the dark, alone? You wouldn't! If a huge tiger is waiting to rip your head off, you go where the tiger ISN'T. Same for a bully as for a tiger. If a bully is waiting to rip your arms off, you go where the bully ISN'T. Don't risk getting hurt. Go somewhere else.

At school, some places are safer than others. If you have to, go to the library at lunchtime—it's quiet and there are usually more teachers than bullies in a library.

## Decide What You Will Say Ahead of Time

When you are being bullied it is hard to know what to say. When you are nervous, it is hard to sound confident. So your best strategy is to decide what to say ahead of time. Practise in front of the bathroom mirror. Keep it simple.

## Look Confident.

What do we know about bullies? They pick on people who look weak. And who looks weak? People with hunched shoulders, people who stare at the ground, people who make no eye contact. Some targets of bullying send out signals. Their voice is weak, they look down a lot.

If you look shy, you are a target. There are things you can do that will help you feel better about yourself. So your mission is to look confident.

Notice how confident people talk, and talk how they talk—clear and loud.

Watch how confident people walk, and walk how they walk.

Straighten your shoulders. Look straight ahead. You can practise this in the bathroom mirror. Head up, chest out. From today, make it a habit to look people in the eye. And guess what—you'll feel better. You'll feel more confident. Fact!

When you change what you do with your body, it changes how you feel. Try this little experiment. Put a big smile on your face, right now. Okay, now close your eyes and think of something sad.

Did you do it? Go on, do it!

What did you discover? It is impossible to keep a smile on your face and think of something sad. You either have to think of something happy or wipe off your smile. That is how strong the link is between your body and your thoughts.

What does this mean? That if you walk like you are confident—with your head up and your chest out, and if you look people in the eye—you will feel happier and stronger.

Bullies will be less likely to pick you as a weak target. If they do start bullying you, and you look confident, they will be more likely to quit—because bullies are cowards.

## Encourage Yourself

Any soccer player, marathon runner, mountain climber knows that to get through a tough situation, you need to encourage yourself.

Athletes continually encourage themselves:
- "I got through this before"
- "forget the insults, stay calm"
- "I can do this, one minute at a time."

To have inner strength like any athlete—you need to do exactly the same.

You might say, "The bullies should leave me alone! I shouldn't have to act confident, I shouldn't have to encourage myself!" That's true. But if you are being bullied, you have to deal with it.

Here's the good news. Thousands of people who were bullied at school become happy and successful adults. And they will tell you, "I decided to become stronger, I found an inner confidence".

## Be Friendly to Other People

Not everyone will be your friend—but you can be friendly to everyone. When you make an effort to be friendly with a lot of kids, three things happen:
- you develop more confidence
- school becomes more enjoyable
- bullies begin to leave you alone.

**Walk to School With A Friend**

Bullies are cowards who only pick a fight when they know they can win. If you are with friends, they are more likely to leave you alone.

Even if your friend is younger than you, bullies will be more likely to leave you alone if you have company.

**Keep a Diary**

Keep a record of the bullying. When you tell a teacher, a friendly adult, or the police, you need to have the facts: when, where and what happened. Keep to the facts. Avoid exaggerating.

You have seen those TV courtroom dramas... the prosecuting attorney stands before the accused, and says, "At approximately 11:15pm on 4th November 2010 you entered Mr Jones' house through the bathroom window. You struck him twice on the back of the head with a blunt object ...

Exhibit A: Here is a photo of Mr Jones' head.

Exhibit B: The ransom note.

Exhibit C: The baseball bat."

The prosecutor has facts: dates, times, people, places, photographs and the

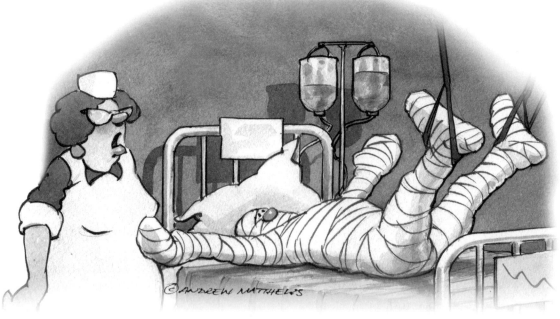

*"Who won?"*

baseball bat. The accused is found guilty based on hard evidence—facts.

But what happens when everyone KNOWS the accused is guilty but there are no facts? The crook goes free! Not enough evidence.

It is the same if you are being bullied. If you want help from a parent, teacher, principal, policeman or a judge, you need to gather evidence. FACTS.

Keep a diary of every bullying incident, it might look like this:

**TIME: 12:25pm, 14 July**
LOCATION: The corridor outside the lunchroom.
INCIDENT: Tanya Jones and Louise Brown approached me from behind. Tanya said, "I'm going to break your face" She pushed me face-first into the lockers.
Attached see doctor's report, doctor's bill, photos of injuries sustained.

**TIME: 4:31pm, 14 July**
INCIDENT: I received an offensive email from Louise Brown. Photocopy attached.

If you want help, you need to help yourself. If you give all the facts to a principal or a policeman, they HAVE TO help you. They are guilty if they don't.

Also, if you are being cyber-bullied:
- save all messages and emails as evidence. Even if you have printed copies, keep the originals in your phone or laptop.
- if the threats are coming through your phone or by email, you may be able to block future contact.
- contact the school. If the threats are coming from your fellow students, or over the school network, the school is obliged to act.

Keep telling people about the problem. If the first adult doesn't help, tell another. If the first policeman doesn't help, tell another. Persist.

## How Can I Like Myself?

I n our hearts, most of us believe we should be doing better. We think that we should have got higher grades. We want to be popular and hang out with the "in" crowd. We feel that we don't measure up to our parents' expectations.

Parents help to confirm this idea when they say things like, "Why can't you be more like your brother?"

Whenever you are feeling low, be your own best friend. Accept that, up to now, you have lived your life the best way you knew how. No one sets out to screw up their life! Like anyone, you've done the odd stupid thing. With more information you'll likely do better in the future.

Liking yourself means forgiving yourself. If you have made some serious mistakes, if you have hurt some people—and yourself—feeling guilty won't help.

If you are feeling guilty about something, you have already suffered enough. Being guilty for another six months won't help anybody.

### Forget perfection and aim for improvement.

It's a funny thing. When you forgive yourself for your own mistakes you automatically begin to let others off the hook for the same things. Which means you begin to enjoy other people more.

### "But I'm not brilliant ..."

You might look at yourself and say, "I'm not as beautiful as my sister, I'm not as talented as my friends and I'm not brilliant at anything! How can I feel good about me?"

Fact: Nobody is good at everything and most of us have those thoughts!

But here's the lowdown! Talent and beauty are very useful—but there are plenty of talented and beautiful people around whom we don't necessarily admire. And some of them are a pain in the butt!

The qualities most of us value above all others are HONESTY, COURAGE,

KINDNESS, PERSISTENCE, GENEROSITY and HUMILITY.

Take a look at this list and you'll find something interesting. You aren't BORN with these things. You DEVELOP them. Anyone can have them! If you want self-respect and respect from others, you don't have to be an Einstein or a super-model.

You simply work at developing your own honesty, determination, generosity, humility, kindness and courage. It is called "character".

## What if No One Else Gives Me Any Praise?

When you are three years old, you need everyone's approval ... "Mummy, Daddy look at me. Look how clever I am!" And Mummy says, "Yes darling! You can poke your tongue out! You must be a genius!"

But growing up we learn to stand on our own feet. With maturity we begin to take more notice of our own opinion and less notice of other people's. It's nice to get praise from other people but it won't always happen. As we get older, we learn to live without it. This is called growing up!

When you get no encouragement or support from anybody else, support yourself. Make a quiet note of your own achievements, make a note of the caring and positive things you do.

Grab a piece of paper, sit down and make a list right now—and when you have made your list, keep it where you can look at it regularly.

## What About People Who Tell You, "I Am the Greatest!"

Don't you hate people who are always trying to impress you ... "My uncle is a multi-millionaire ... my father drives a Ferrari ... I know the president ... my best friend has a big yacht". Some people will tell you, "I am the smartest", "I am the richest", "I am the most beautiful". This is not evidence of a good self-image.

People who keep telling you how wonderful they are have little confidence. People who keep telling you how clever they are or how rich they are or how many famous friends they have usually don't like themselves very much. So their strategy is, "If I can get you to like me, then maybe I can get to like myself."

Extraordinary people don't have to keep telling you, "I'm amazing!"

Does Batman say, "Look at me! I'm incredible and I have the fastest wheels in town"? No. He knows he's cool. So he just gets about saving Gotham City. Does

James Bond tell everyone, "I'm sexy and brave"? No. He knows he's brave. He just fights the crooks.

These guys just make it happen. When you know something in your heart—when you really believe it—you don't need anyone to agree with you. You know it and that's enough.

It's the people that don't have much—and can't do much—that talk the most. My mother always told me, "Empty barrels make the most noise". If you understand why people boast, then they don't irritate you so much.

## But Do I REALLY Need To Like Myself?

Yes! People who don't like themselves are a pain in the neck!

Usually, people with a poor self-image use one of two irritating strategies—they either:

a) criticise you a lot—which is what bullies do, or

b) they criticise themselves a lot.

**STRATEGY A:** They criticise you a lot. They figure that by criticising other people they can feel better about themselves.

Let's take Fred, who feels inferior. Fred thinks he has a big nose and piggy eyes. He also secretly feels a bit stupid.

So what's his strategy to feel better about himself? He criticises all his friends. He has names for them like "Flathead", "Chicken Legs" and "Dogbrain". Whenever someone else makes a mistake, he announces it to the whole class. (He probably doesn't even realise he criticises people—or why he does it).

If you have parents, friends or brothers and sisters who don't like themselves—they might criticise you and everyone around them. Just remember that they criticise you because they have a problem. If you remember that they are actually hurting inside you won't get so upset by their behaviour.

**STRATEGY B:** Some people who don't like themselves criticise themselves a lot. They use reverse psychology ...

Take Mary who doesn't like herself. She's always telling you, "You are prettier than me. You are smarter. Nobody likes me." She's hoping that you will reply, "No Mary! You are clever. You are beautiful." After a while, people like Mary get on your nerves!

**IN A NUTSHELL**

When we don't like ourselves, we irritate other people. We also put ourselves through a lot of stress. When we accept ourselves a little better, we don't play these games.

## Your Self-Image

Imagine this story ... during your first weeks of school, you are sitting in maths class gazing out the window when the teacher asks you, "What's the answer?"

"What's the answer?" You don't even know the question! You are speechless. Your face turns red. Panic and tears. At that moment you tell yourself, "I hate mathematics!"

That night your mother asks: "How was school?"

You say: "I couldn't answer the maths question."

And Mother says: "But no one in our family can do maths!"

Suddenly you breathe a huge sigh of relief ... "Of course I hate multiplication! It's in my genes!" From that day onward, it's official. Will you ever look forward to mathematics again? Not likely! Now you begin to tell your friends, "I hate maths. My entire family is bad with numbers!" You figure, "Why make an effort? I'll never conquer it."

But what REALLY happened here? You got a bad start and fell behind.

Maybe this mathematics story didn't happen to you. But most of us have our own story—about singing, hitting a ball, drawing a picture, learning to swim, speaking in front of the class. We got a bad start and fell behind. No one came along to encourage us. After one embarrassing experience we gradually convinced ourselves, "It's hopeless!"

It's worth examining where we get these "facts" about what we can do and what we can't do. Usually these "facts" are simply beliefs we have—and they are based on very shaky evidence. Teachers, parents, brothers, cousins tell us things about ourselves when we are young. When we are six years old—or ten years old—we believe it … "This is Mary—she's not academic." "This is Rudy—he's the naughty one." "This is Frank—he'll be fat like his father."

Then we spend a lifetime believing something someone told us that's not true.

If you have labels on yourself, like "I am a slow learner", "I am uncoordinated", "I can't multiply" ask yourself, "What's the proof?"

**IN A NUTSHELL**

Challenge your labels. When we give ourselves a second chance, and get some help, most often WE CAN DO IT!

People change. You can change.

## Feeling Good

When we are feeling good about ourselves, we feel healthier, we have more energy and problems don't seem so overwhelming.

When we are feeling miserable—or when we don't like ourselves—it is almost like we punish ourselves. We binge on junk food or go looking for arguments. It is not that we do it consciously, but it happens.

On those gloomy days we are much more likely to fall off ladders or trip over the carpet. Even accidents just seem to happen when we are feeling sad.

So, how do you keep feeling good about yourself?

1. Never criticise yourself. We all have faults but you don't need to advertise yours. Always speak well of yourself.

2. Accept compliments. When someone pays you a compliment treat it as a gift. Say, "Thank you".

3. Give more compliments. There is a myth that if you pay compliments to

MATTHEWS

other people, they will get a big head and then you will feel worse. The fact is, we always feel a lot better.

> 66 When you make a mistake be sure to say, "I made a mistake" and not "I am a mistake." 99

4. Separate your behaviour from yourself. Everyone makes mistakes. When you make a mistake be sure to say, "I made a mistake" and not "I am a mistake".

5. Spend time with positive people. The company you keep has a huge effect on how you feel. If your family aren't happy and uplifting, then you will need to find friends who are happy and supportive.

6. Continually play movies in your mind of how you want to be. Wake up ten minutes earlier and picture how you want your day to be. If you repeatedly play movies of yourself as confident, happy and successful, you will become more like that. It is the law of the mind. Whatever you think about you become.

**In a Nutshell**
How you feel about yourself is in your hands.

## Making Friends

### Blaming Other People

There is always something you can do to make your life better. If you are being bullied, if you have no friends, there are things you can do.

Fred says, "I haven't got any friends. Nobody understands me!" That's avoiding responsibility. While Fred blames everyone else, he'll have a lot of lonely Saturday nights.

Mary says, "I know I'm miserable. It's my mother's fault." That's a recipe for more misery. Blaming your mother doesn't help.

Whenever you fail at something, ask yourself, "Was I partly responsible for this? How can I make sure this doesn't happen again?" These are questions successful people ask themselves.

It's not what happens to you, it's how you see it—and how you fix it.

## What Others Think

Rule # 1: Not everyone will agree with you.

Rule # 2: It's okay.

Rule # 3: Not everyone will like you.

Rule # 4: That's okay too. You won't die!

Do you care what other people think? Sure! We all do. We all want other people to think we are cool, smart, attractive and fun. But some people won't like you. What do you do? Get over it!

## Trying Too Hard

Why do we love babies? It's partly because babies don't care whether you like them or not? Babies eat, scream, make noises and make smells, and they don't care.

Babies don't try to impress people. When you are a baby, you don't have to be cool or intelligent or sexy or smart.

Isn't it fascinating! Babies don't care what we think about them—and we love them for it.

There is something to learn from this. Be yourself. This doesn't mean you should be rude or selfish. It does mean there's such a thing as trying too hard.

## Being Scared of People

Has this ever happened to you? There's a new kid in school—we'll call him Joe.

On Joe's first day you see him in the corridor, and you want to say, "Hello!" But you think to yourself, "I'll only say 'Hello' if he says 'Hello' first".

But he doesn't say "Hello" so you don't say "Hello", and at the end of the day you say to yourself, "He's not very friendly!" Next day you decide, "I'll say 'Hello', but only if he does". But Joe doesn't speak, so you don't.

By the third day, you start playing games. You pretend not to notice each other. You pass him in the corridor—he pretends to look at the ceiling, you pretend to study the floor.

After a week, you say to yourself, "He's a jerk—I don't like him anyway".

Meanwhile, what was Joe thinking all the time? "I'll say 'Hello' if he says 'Hello'". While you were scared to talk to Joe, he was scared to talk to you!

On the outside people often look very cool. But nobody is as confident as they look. On the inside they worry about all the things you might worry about ... "Am I smart enough? Am I slim enough? Have I got a big nose?"

**In a Nutshell**
You don't need to be scared of people. Half the time, they are scared of you!

## Forgiving People

Let's say some guy called Steven bullied you for six months. Steven slashed your bicycle tyres, stole your skateboards, threw your books onto the roof. Steven made your life hell.

> 66 *Where do we get the idea that if WE don't forgive people, THEY suffer?* 99

You spoke to your teachers and Steven was persuaded to leave you alone. What should you do now? The best thing you can do is move on. Forget the whole thing.

Now some people might say, "NO WAY! I will never forget, I will never forgive! I will resent that guy for the rest of my life!" But then who suffers? Not Steven!

You're pacing the floor. You've got the knot in your stomach. You're losing sleep. Steven is probably at the movies!

Where do we get the idea that if WE don't forgive people, THEY suffer? It's nuts!

When you refuse to forgive people—your mother, your teachers, your boss—you wither up inside. It wrecks YOUR life! Next time you are resenting someone, close your eyes and experience your feelings. Experience your body. Making people guilty makes you miserable.

Miserable people keep a list of resentments in their head ... "she let me down, he talked behind my back, he lied ..." They run through it to check that nothing is missing! They add to the list.

Happy people have better things to do.

To forgive someone, you don't have to agree with what they did. You just have to want your life to work.

Sometimes we say, "I'll forgive but I won't forget." Which means "I'll let it go for the moment, but I might want to remind you about it from time to time". To forgive is to let something go.

Studies at the Public Health Institute in California confirm that hostility and resentment tear down your immune system and double your risk of heart attack, cancer and all kinds of illness. Bitterness makes you sick!

One more thing about forgiving people—it's a continuous process. If you want to be happy, you'll be continually letting go of things—erasing people from your list.

**In a Nutshell**
Is forgiveness easy? Usually not. But you don't forgive people for their benefit. You do it for your benefit.

## Drugs

If you have been bullied a lot, you may have thought, "Perhaps drugs would ease the pain. Other people do it". Consider this:

Imagine you had a friend whose hobby was hitting himself over the head with a hammer. Would you say to yourself, "I need to try that!"

Would you say, "Give me that hammer! Let me hit myself a couple of times so I know how it feels!" No!

Would you say, "I want to try it to be sure?" You wouldn't! Some things you know are stupid without trying them. Without trying it you know it is stupid to stand in front of an oncoming train. You just know!

Without trying them, you can tell that drugs will ruin your life.

Perhaps you've seen drug addicts interviewed on television. The conversation usually goes something like this ...

Q: "How much have you spent on this stuff?"

A: "Everything I had! Ten thousand, twenty thousand, a hundred thousand ..."

Q: "How does it feel?"

A: "I've lost my car, job, family, friends, I can't eat, I feel sick every day, my body aches all over."

Q: "How did you start?"

A: "Smoking grass! Then I tried other stuff."

Usually, the story is something like, "I had this friend, Dave, and he was no junkie. I was feeling a bit depressed and he offered me this stuff. He said it would make me feel better. I thought I could handle it ... I never knew it would lead to this."

They never thought it would wreck their lives.

You may have friends who offer you all kinds of nasty things. And when you refuse, they may get angry or irritated and call you "a chicken"—and worse. But remember that everyone secretly admires strength. If you have the guts to say,

"No", and continue to say "No", you will have their respect—because you can do something they couldn't. (Though they may never admit it).

**In a Nutshell**

Every drug addict "thought they could handle it". They all said something like, "I'll just try it once so I know". It's like hitting yourself with a hammer. It's like walking in front of a train. You don't need to try it to see if it's good for you.

ANDREW MATTHEWS

# Not my Child!

## 8

## "So What if My Kid is a Bully?"

Parents of bullies often deny what is happening. Maybe they think, "It's not my problem!" But long term, bullying is just as much a problem for the bullies.

In the USA, ordinary eight-year-old children have a 1 in 20 chance of having a criminal record by the age of 30. For eight-year-old bullies the odds are 1 in 4.

In other words, an eight-year-old bully is five times more likely to have a criminal record by age 30. [7]

Childhood bullies are more likely to be convicted of serious crimes.

Bullies who refine their skills as kids become bullying boyfriends, bullying bosses and bullying dads.

### Brisbane Radio 97.3FM

In Brisbane, Australia, radio station 97.3FM runs a yearly campaign to reduce bullying. Says breakfast host Robyn Bailey, "Our campaign is run over a week and has the full support of both the Queensland and National Education departments. It has now become an annual feature on all school calendars and each school runs their own programs leading up to the day.

"In 2011 the Say No To Bullying Day was recognised as a national campaign by the Human Rights Commission which sent a letter of support. The idea is to get kids, parents and teachers to work together to recognise bullying and do something about it. Each year there is a different theme. In 2010 it was about bystanders and the part they play in enabling bullying."

**MATT'S STORY:** During the 97.3FM 2011 Bullying Awareness Week, Matt, an irate father, called Robin and co-host Terry Hansen to tell his story. Matt recalled, "As a child I got bullied to the point … where I stopped wearing glasses. It's now affected my eye sight. I can only drive in daylight hours."

He then explained that a few weeks earlier, he had been told by school officials that his teenagers were bullying another child. Matt's children repeatedly denied the accusation.

Matt was so disturbed by the news that he set out to discover the truth.

He continued to tell the listeners: "Yesterday afternoon I'm on my way home ... come 'round the corner three streets from home [and] there's my 17-year-old son and my 15-year-old daughter and they are fair beating the living crap out of this kid," he said.

"I pulled up, I damaged the car [as] I put the car up the gutter. I grabbed a hold of both of them, threw them in the back of the car, got the young kid that they were beating up ... took him home to his parents [and] marched both my kids into the local police station. "

"They have both now been charged with assault."

Matt explained that his children were bullying the 13-year-old because he wore glasses. The parents of the bullied boy called him the same evening to tell him their son's jaw was broken during the assault.

Matt admitted that his children had not spoken to him since the incident. Matt said that he and his wife would stand behind the parents of the target if they decided to pursue damages.

> ❝ How can a father turn his own children in to the police? ❞

Matt explained that as punishment he had taken his son's car and his daughter's horse away from them—and the car and horse would be sold immediately as part of their punishment.

Some days later Robin and Terry followed up with Matt. Matt revealed that his children were now remorseful for the incident, understood how wrong it was—and wanted the proceeds from the sale of the horse and car to be given to the parents of the injured boy.

When questioned about turning his kids in to the police, he said: "I will admit it was a hard thing to do to take my kids to a police station. If I had to do it again, I don't think I could." But he said he knew he had done the right thing, "There was no excuse for what they did".

The response of listeners was overwhelming. Matt became a hero to many—and a villain.

Most parents will say, "A bully? Not my child!" yet here was a father who was prepared to admit the truth and take action.

And of course, others were stunned and disgusted, "How can a father turn his own children in to the police?"

The story spread through the newspapers and across the internet.
Did Matt do the right thing?

- He took the trouble to discover the truth.
- He admitted that his kids were bullies.
- He made it clear to his children that their behaviour was wrong.
- He made sure there were consequences.
- He offered support to the bullied boy and his family.

**KATIE'S STORY:** *In 2003, Katie Jarvis wrote a piece on bullying for a UK national newspaper:*

### There Must Be Some Mistake!

It all came out of the blue. I got a phone call one day from another parent saying "This behaviour has got to stop!", I was completely taken aback. What behaviour? My son? Surely some mistake?

After all, I had a bright child from a happy family and he seemed to have plenty of friends. I was sceptical that my nine-year-old could really be in the wrong.

There was name-calling, intimidation and stone-throwing—the usual unacceptable behaviour. As it turned out it was my boy who was doing the bullying.

It's comforting to believe that bullies belong to someone else—that they are deprived children from dysfunctional families.

The truth is that you can't neatly divide the world into aggressors and victims. Many children have the potential to be the school bully, even my beloved son. For a parent that can be a pretty devastating discovery.

### "Tell Me About It"

I started to question him - softly, softly. "Anything you'd like to talk to me about? How was school today?" "Fine".

So I moved on to asking about specific incidents. "Is it true you threw a stone at someone today?" I have to admit I was unreasonably comforted when he replied: "Yes, but he threw one first." It was only when the school became involved and told me it was my son causing the problems that I started to take it in.

How could I deal with the situation? After all, I couldn't be at school when the incidents were taking place and no matter how much I talked to my son—reasoned and at times even pleaded with him—he didn't seem to see what was happening in the same light.

Looking at it from an adult perspective, I can see now that his incentives were few. If you're a victim of bullying, you want to work to alter the situation. You desperately need things to change. If you're the bully, on the other hand, you have the power and the control and, for a child of nine, that can feel pretty good. Put more specifically, the victim would cry every morning and ask not to go to school, while my son went quite happily…

The whole episode lasted nearly four months—long, long months—and, in the end, it was patience and understanding that paid off. It took a three-way partnership between me, the school and the other parent. In a supreme effort of self-control, my husband and I never shouted at our son or blamed him. We simply tried to get him to see the effect his behaviour was having. Maybe it worked; maybe the situation resolved itself. Who can tell?…

> 66 *In a supreme effort of self-control, my husband and I never shouted at our son or blamed him.* 99

### What I Learned

Of the two of us—my son and me—I think I have been the more affected. For the whole of one term, I crept into the playground at home time, convinced that every other parent hated me, that they thought our home life held shameful secrets, that I was an appalling mother, that my husband beat our children. I'm sure now that they thought nothing of the sort, but paranoia comes easily in those circumstances…

I know I've learnt from the experience. The most important lesson is to admit and to accept responsibility. My children are adored, but they're not perfect.

So many people are willing to say their child is being bullied. But where are all the perpetrators? They must exist, and it's a fair bet that most of them have parents.

I was listening to friends talking the other day about what a hard time their son was having because he was being picked on at school. "Actually," someone confided to me afterwards, "it's their son who's doing the bullying. But try telling them that."

I can understand their reluctance to believe it. But let's face it—it's not only the victims who need to talk about the subject. The only way to stamp out school bullying is for the culprits—and their parents—to put their hands up, too.

> **" So many people are willing to say their child is being bullied. But where are all the perpetrators? "**

Katie hoped that by speaking out as a parent of a bully she would encourage open discussion amongst parents:

I hoped that by speaking out, I'd persuade more people to come forward and say: "Hey! My child is being accused of bullying. Instead of denying it – 'My child would NEVER do such a thing' – I want to be part of the solution. But I don't want to be labelled and accused. I want us all to be on the same side, working towards a solution for everyone."

My plan didn't work.

I was criticised in an education blog that completely missed my point. I received plenty of letters from parents whose children were being bullied. But no parent joined me in admission of 'guilt'.

My child was a normal one who had indulged in a short period of very bad behaviour. Indeed, I was trying to say that my story was more depressingly ordinary than shocking.

My son is now 18, and a fine, upright young man who is about to study at a prestigious university. He has a wonderful girlfriend, a close circle of friends, and is passionate about caring for animals. He can also be awkward, sharp-tongued and sometimes thoughtless. So can I. In other words, he's a normal human being. I love him as he is.

His, so far, has been a success story. Sadly, I can't say the same about bullying.

Until we get people being open about this, we'll never solve it.

## Take Action

How many parents of bullies admit that their child tortures other kids? Not many! How many parents of bullies take action? Not enough.

Not all bullies come from poor families! Professionals sometimes figure: "I'm a surgeon, I'm a lawyer—so my kids aren't bullies!" One executive remarked, "I pay enough money to the school! They should fix the problem!"

Most bullying happens at school because that is where children spend most of their time—mixing with a whole variety of kids they didn't choose to be with. The bullying happens in the school but the seeds of the behaviour are sown at home.

No school can fix what parents won't.

A mother whose son was bullying the kid next door honestly explained to Julie, "My six-year-old, Tom, was called to the principal's office for thumping Allan. He and some other boys punched Allan in the stomach. Apparently my Tom was the ringleader. The neighbours are all gossiping about it. It is so embarrassing."

Julie asked, "How did you deal with it?" The mother said, "Thankfully I didn't need to. Allan's parents are moving to another town."

Amazing! You cure your son's bullying by waiting for your neighbours to move house—and pretend that the problem is fixed.

Here's what's interesting. Even when parents talk of neighbours' children who are bullies, they whisper—as if it's a crime to even discuss it.

People used to whisper about cancer. It is no shame to have cancer—and you don't beat it by pretending that you haven't got it. It's the same with having a bully in the family. You admit it and deal with it.

Kids experiment. They try on different roles— they try to figure out who they are and what behaviour is acceptable or popular. A nine-year-old may try being the bookworm, the class clown or the bully. It doesn't mean he is evil! It doesn't mean his parents have failed.

**In a Nutshell**
There is no shame in having a child that's a bully.
The shame is in ignoring it.

## "I Was the School Bully"

I don't really know how to explain things. I never even realized how awful I was at school until I was at least 22. One day one of the managers at work told me that his daughter had been at the same school as me. She used to dread meeting me at school and she said that I was well known as the school bully. I'd never really admitted to myself that what I did was bullying – it was just a bit of fun as far as I was concerned. I was embarrassed that the manager talked to me. I wanted to drop through the floor. But it made me think about what I had done all those years ago.

> **"** *I liked the feeling of power that bullying gave me.* **"**

It's not that my childhood was so awful. Yes, my parents were always fighting, and my brother picked on me all the time. But I guess lots of kids have stories like that to tell about their lives. I really didn't have much excuse to do what I did, but I liked the feeling of power that bullying gave me. No one messed with me!

I think the bullying started when somebody upset me in the Infants and some of the boys showed me how to make a fist and 'sort her out'. I suppose I just carried on from there. I never used a gang for support and I picked on boys and girls – it didn't matter who they were. I'd lie in wait for them on the way home. I used to cat call and fight them – not just pulling hair and scratching but real fighting. I even knocked a girl out once. I was never beaten. Perhaps I would have stopped if someone had been able to beat me.

I always had an excuse for why I bullied. Things like 'they were snobs' or 'they'd hurt me' but I know they were pathetic excuses. The lads used to egg me on as well but even when we moved to another area, I still carried on. The bullying went on until I left school.

I used to feel a rush whenever I got at someone. I seemed to get satisfaction from knowing that I'd hurt and beaten others. At heart, I was scared. I thought nobody liked me. I thought I was ugly. I had a big nose and the boys all used to tease me. I felt very insecure about how I looked, but then again lots of people feel that way and never bully others.

I am writing to you in the hope that some young bully might read this and change his or her ways before it is too late. Now I feel really bad about what I did, but I wonder if any of my victims will ever know?

Reprinted with permission of Kidscape: www.kidscape.org.uk

*"He hit my bat with his nose!"*

## "Give Me the Facts"

*"Young people learn best when they focus on how they feel about their actions rather than how adults feel."*
**Stan Davis**

Bullies have a way of avoiding the truth – "her stomach came up and hit my foot", "I was walking past when she fell on my fist", "he started it anyway"...

Some bullies are great actors, and will pretend to be totally innocent. Whether you are a parent or a teacher, your job is to encourage bullies to take responsibility—no blame, no excuses, just the truth. So:

- "I pushed her because she made a stupid face", becomes "I pushed her".
- "He started it" becomes "I kicked him in the head".

What else might you say to a bully?

- Tell me exactly what happened.
- I don't care who started it, tell me what you did.
- You didn't have to thump him. You chose to thump him.
- How do you think he feels?
- How can you repair the situation?

Once the child has admitted to bullying, you can help him explore his own reasons for why he does it:

- What were you trying to achieve? Was it for fun? For attention?
- What else could you have done?
- Is there anything worrying you that is causing you to bully?
- Why do you bully? What would help you to stop?

You can't make bullies change. But you can make punishments predictable.

# No Innocent Bystanders

## 9

## Kids Learn to Accept Bullying

*"When everybody stands and watches, you feel you deserve it."*

In 2006 Stan Davis and his colleagues conducted a survey of over 1400 children between kindergarten and 12th grade. Students were asked to complete the following statement:

When I see someone being teased or hit I think:

    a) THEY DESERVE IT, or

    b) THEY DON'T DESERVE IT.

As you can see in the graph below, 93% of kindergarten kids had sympathy for the bullied child. By age 16 or 17, only sixty five percent had sympathy for the bullied child. [8]

| | Percentage | |
|---|---|---|
| Grades K–4 | 93 | 7 |
| Grades 5–8 | 77 | 23 |
| Grades 9–12 | 65 | 35 |

☐ They don't deserve it  ■ They deserve it

MATHEWS

**In a Nutshell**

The older children get, the more likely they are to say, "Bullied kids deserve what they get." If adults and classmates take no action, children may learn to accept that bullying is okay.

**What Would You Do?**

As adults it is easy to say, "Children who witness bullying should do something to stop it!" But we may be seeing things from an adult point of view.

As an adult, it is easier to stop young children bullying. As an adult:

- you have some experience in resolving conflict
- you don't care whether some ten-year-old bully is going to like you
- you aren't going to lose any friends if you make a stand, and
- you aren't worried that this ten-year-old is going to beat you up tomorrow!

But put yourself in a situation where you are less confident...

Imagine you are sitting on a train late at night. Suddenly, at the far end of the carriage, four big strong guys burst through the door. These guys have lots of earrings and tattoos but few teeth. They are holding a fifth young man—one has him in a headlock, another has one arm behind his back. It seems they know each other.

The bullies grab his boots and toss them out the window. One takes his bag. One says, "You dumb F#** we're going to teach you a lesson." You are at the far end of the carriage but you can smell the fear.

No phone call to police is going to save this guy now—somebody needs to take action. Twenty other commuters do nothing. They are all closer to the incident than you.

Would you:

- Run to help the bullied guy?
- Tell yourself, "He probably deserves it! Maybe he stole their wallets!"
- Feel thankful that you were at the other end of the carriage and breathe a sigh of relief when they all got off the train?

Not so easy to be the courageous bystander now!

# Why I used to be a Bully

**Angus Watson spent his schooldays tormenting the weak. He explains why he did it and how he stopped.**

From the ages of 9 to 11 I was a bully. Anyone in my year or below who looked different, sounded funny, smelt odd or acted differently from the rest of us was fair game for physical and mental attacks. If I wasn't the main bully, I was certainly a ringleader.

Bullying tactics ranged from the psychological—constantly reminding somebody that they were fat, smelly, foreign or gay, or all four, to physical—pricking them with compasses, head-butting them, or giving them dead arms.

There was one boy, Edmund Jones, who had giant ears, yellow skin, smelt of urine and whose father was the mild-mannered French teacher. Unfortunately, because of this cruel combination of circumstances, he got it.

One day, Bill Davis, my impressive friend from the year above, came into our classroom. There were three of us there, and Jones.

"What are you doing?" Davis asked.

"We're trying to make Jones cry just by teasing him." I answered.

"That's not how to make Jones cry," he replied, picking up Jones's cheap, heavy briefcase. He ran around all the desks gathering speed and stopped just before Jones and let go of the case. It hit Jones in the midriff like a battering ram and burst open in an explosion of paper, books, conkers and sweet wrappers.

"That's how you make Jones cry," said Davis as Jones ran from the room sobbing.

I was awed by Davis' style and inventiveness. From that day, I raised my game. Bullying took on a crueller and more imaginative twist. Breaking expensive pencils while their owners watched, teasing them about their mothers' hairstyles, throwing sticks dipped in sheep-poo at them, and so on. Pretty horrible stuff, and certainly nothing to remember with pride. So why did I do it?

Other than the fact that I was plain nasty, it was part of my childhood culture. My big brother whacked me with happy regularity, as did all my dormitory captains at boarding school. One particular prefect would make us drink water until we were sick. Another made my friend cut me with an army tin opener.

My friends and I used to stab each other, and ourselves, with compasses for amusement. We used to spray deodorant from very close on to our skin, making it blister. I still have scars from that. Pain was all around. Bullying, I suppose, was a way of passing this on to the weaker boys.

I stopped when I was 12, I think, because I met girls. My parents bought a holiday house in the Isle of Wight with another family. They had twin daughters my age. My attempts to impress them and their friends by hurting smaller people were pathetic and they told me as much. So I stopped being a bully. At least, looking back, it seems that's what did it. Maybe I just grew up.

Do I feel remorse? Not really. Well, maybe a smidgen. It sounds cliched, but I feel the people I bullied grew up tougher, and more determined to prove themselves. Also, I was a completely different person then.

What made Angus Watson suddenly stop bullying weaker kids?
- Did his parents beat him until he couldn't walk?
- Did the principal suspend him for a month?
- Did he find God?

No. He found two girls who told him hurting smaller people was pathetic.

Here is the problem with bullying:

1. Most bullies are quite happy with their behaviour. They have power and attention and they are popular within a group.
2. Most targets of bullying believe that bullying is inevitable. They think they deserve it.
3. Most bullying goes undetected by parents and teachers. How can adults

ANDREW MATTHEWS

discipline children for things they don't know about?

Angus Watson's story perfectly illustrates who holds the most power. It's not the bully, it's not the target. It's the BYSTANDERS.

For bullies the payoff is power and popularity. Bullies value *getting attention* much more than *being kind*. Why should a bully change—until what he values most disappears.

> **66** *Bullies value getting attention much more than being kind.* **99**

In the movie *Seventeen Again*, Mike confronts Stan the bully in the school cafeteria. The hall packed with students falls silent as Mike makes his speech:

> "Stan is a bully. Why? It'd be way too easy to say Stan preys on the weak simply because he's a dick. No... no... Stan here is much more complex than that.
>
> See, according to leading psychiatrists, Stan is a bully for one of three reasons...
>
> One... underneath all that male bravado, there's an insecure little girl banging on the closet door trying to get out.
>
> Two... like a caveman, Stan's brain is underdeveloped. Therefore, Stan is unable to use self-control. And so he acts out aggressively.
>
> Three... Stan has a small wiener."

Within a minute Stan has lost his fan club. Problems are more easily solved in Disney movies—but the scene underlines what works in real life.

Bullying is about politics. Bullies want popularity. Bullies need supporters. When the supporters—or bystanders—withdraw their vote, it's over for the bully.

## Why Blame the Target?

When you ask a class of children, "Who gets bullied here and why do they get bullied?" you get answers like:

- Jim is bullied because he is fat.
- Mary gets teased because she is slow.
- Tim is bullied because he wears weird clothes and talks like a faggot.
- Jane is bullied because she is beautiful.

Bystanders don't say, 'Tim is bullied because the bullies choose to bully—and if the bullies didn't choose Tim they would choose someone else."

The children don't say, "Tim gets bullied because the bullies are bigots."

Onlookers are quick to decide, "THE BULLIED KID NEEDS TO CHANGE HIS BEHAVIOUR".

Bystanders rarely say, "The bullies make the choice to be mean. It isn't Tim's fault".

### Bullying is No Different to Racism

If a person is being abused for being black, we recognise it is wrong. We don't say to the black person, "You must be doing something to create the problem! Pretend it doesn't worry you! Or stop being black!"

We don't expect the black person to change. We hold the bigot responsible.

These days we recognise that a woman has the right to work in an environment where she isn't touched and abused. We don't say to a woman who is being harassed, "Just pretend it doesn't worry you". We don't expect the woman to change. We hold the offender responsible.

But with bullying? We haven't evolved that far. We acknowledge that bullying is not acceptable—but then we say to the target, "Behave differently! Pretend you don't mind being ridiculed. Don't carry money".

Even in this book I offer advice to targets of bullying—but targets of bullying shouldn't have to change.

### In a Nutshell
When will things get better? When bystanders become upstanders.

## When Bystanders Do Nothing

*"If no one does anything, you start to believe that what the bullies say is true."*

Bystanders are quick to give advice. "Jim should stand up to the bullies. Mary should fight back!"

Here's a message for the bystanders: "HOW DO YOU EXPECT AN ISOLATED, INTIMIDATED LITTLE KID TO STAND UP FOR HIMSELF WHEN YOU WON'T STAND UP FOR HIM?"

*"To the world you may be just one person... but to one person you might be the world."*
Mark Twain

**Excuses**

There are many reasons why decent children will stand by and watch one of their peers being bullied. Excuses include:

"**He deserves it.** If he wasn't so strange the bullies would leave him alone. If he wasn't such a dork, if he didn't wear such dumb clothes, if he wasn't such a nerd, geek, faggot, and anyway, maybe he asked for it."

"**It is none of my business.**" When the neighbours are hurling insults and dinner plates at each other, you may decide that it is not your fight. In the same way, when your daughter sees bullying she may decide, "It is not pretty but it is not my problem."

"**You want me to rat on other kids? Are you crazy?**"

"**He's a cry-baby. It will toughen him up.**" Kids reason that an emotional child will benefit from rough treatment. Far from toughening them up, it often breaks them down.

**"The bully is my friend."** For some children it is difficult to make friends and keep them. Imagine that your twelve-year-old son had been lonely and friendless. Finally he has a friend, Barry—a kid who used to bully him.

In the school corridors your son notices Barry the Bully teasing some other kid. Is your son going to take a moral stand and risk losing his only friend?

**"I could lose ALL my friends!"** Bullies often rule by popularity or by fear. If your son takes on the bully, he could lose not just the bully's friendship, but all his friends.

**"It is not my problem. Stay out of it!"** Children hear their parents say this all the time!

**"If I confront the bully he might beat ME up!** I could also lose all my teeth."Bystanders sometimes assume that the only way to help a bullied child is for them to start throwing punches at the bully. There are better ways for bystanders to help a bullied child than to get into a fist fight with the bully.

**"I don't know what to do!"**

### Are You a Bystander or an Upstander?

In 2007 a grade nine student arrived for his first day at Central Kings Rural High School, Nova Scotia, wearing a pink shirt. The boy was physically threatened, taunted, called "faggot".

When grade twelve students Travis Price and David Shepherd heard of the bullying, they decided to make a stand. Price and Shepherd visited a local discount store and bought every pink shirt the store had. Then they launched an overnight campaign via email and social networking sites telling all their friends, "Wear pink tomorrow".

Next day Central Kings High was a sea of pink—hundreds of students had joined the cause.

Said Price, 'I learned that two people can come up with an idea, run with it, and it can do wonders. Finally, someone stood up for a weaker kid. The bullies were never heard from again."

The idea of wearing pink shirts to make a stand against bullying spread to over 60 schools in Nova Scotia and then across Canada.

### In a Nutshell
You can fight bullying without fighting the bully.

MATTHEWS

**What Can You Do as a Bystander?**

*"Every time bystanders act effectively to stop bullying, they see their own potential to make a positive impact on the world."*
Stan Davis

When you see other people being bullied, and do nothing, you send a message to the bully that it is okay with you. You also send a message to the target that they deserve it. So what can you do?

**Tell the bully to stop it.** You might say something like:

"Please leave her alone."

"You have no right to pick on him".

**Ask the target of the bullying to leave the scene with you.** The toughest part about being bullied is feeling all alone. You can offer support to a bullied child by helping them to leave the scene. You say, "Come on, let's go," and you walk away WITH THEM.

**Be a friend to the person who is being bullied.** A friendly face or a pat on the back means the world to a child who is feeling worthless and scared. Just saying, "How are you doing?" or "Let's eat lunch together" makes all the difference to a bullied kid.

**Chat with the bullied child.** Show you care. "Have you told a teacher?" Help the target to see a) that the bullying is not okay and b) parents, teachers or police should be told.

**Take the bullied child to see a teacher.** For reasons we all understand, bullied kids don't tell teachers. But if you offer to go along too, and tell the teacher what you saw happen, you give the bullied child confidence to speak up.

**Encourage the bullied child to tell others.** Ask, "Do your parents know about this? If it is really serious, "You need to tell your parents and you need to tell the police. How can I help?"

**"Everybody Does It"**

Typical problem: James is being beaten and threatened at school. James would like to ask his teachers for help but he says, "Everyone thinks it's wrong to *snitch*."

In fact, everyone doesn't think it's wrong—not even close to everyone! In fact, 75% of the students in James' class think that a bullied kid should tell his teachers. But James doesn't know the facts—so he keeps quiet.

These are real figures from a real school. Three quarters of the class said, "Bullied kids should tell the teachers". But bullied kids like James don't know they have the support of their classmates. So they suffer in silence.

### What Kids Really Think

There is a technique to help James and the silent majority and it is called Social Norms. It's a simple idea.

Here's how it works:

1. You survey a class of students who say, "I don't tell my teachers about bullying because everybody knows it's not okay to snitch".
2. In the survey you ask them the question: "If you are being bullied, do YOU think it is okay to tell the teacher?"
3. The results reveal that most students think a bullied kid should tell the teacher. You then reveal the results of your survey: 75% OF OUR STUDENTS SAY THAT A BULLIED CHILD SHOULD TELL THE TEACHERS. The students are very surprised.
4. You publicise the results all over the school. You include the information in your orientations, you post the statistics on the screen savers of the school's computers, you hang posters in the hallways.
5. Knowing they have the support of their peers, a chunk of teenagers change their behavior.

This strategy has been used with success to combat binge drinking on American college campuses. When college students discover that more than half the student body thinks that binge drinking is stupid, about 10% change their behaviour. It saves a lot of brain cells.

The same principle can work with bullying.

## Choose Your Friends Carefully

Did you ever race into a public toilet that smelt so bad you wanted to choke? But you were so desperate to go to the bathroom that you had no choice.

Did you notice something? By the time you left five minutes later, it didn't smell quite so bad!

And what if you accidentally locked yourself in there for an hour? You'd be saying, "What smell?"

What's the principle here? That WE GET USED TO WHATEVER ENVIRONMENT WE'RE IN.

If you don't smoke, and no one around you smokes, you never even think of smoking. But if all your friends smoke, and you hang out in smoky bars, you get used to it. Sooner or later you're smoking!

If your friends tell lies, in the beginning it worries you. After a while, you get used to the fact that some people tell lies. Hang out with them long enough and you begin telling lies.

Hang out with miserable people, you become miserable—and you think it's normal! Mix with critical people, you become critical—and you think its normal.

If you join a group of friends that makes fun of other kids' clothes and hair, and sends nasty text messages and emails—then, in the beginning it will worry you. But spend enough time with them and you'll start bullying other kids too.

Now here is the good news. If you hang out with friends who are happy and motivated, then you become happy and motivated—and you think that is normal.

Don't kid yourself that you aren't affected by your friends.

If your family or friends are negative and miserable, then you will need to find some positive, happy friends. Somewhere in your life, you must have some positive company—or the pessimists and bullies will drag you down—and you won't even know it's happening.

**In a Nutshell**

Every day we are affected and infected by the people and attitudes around us. Sometimes we need to take action—or change friends—while we can still say, "Something smells around here!"

## "The Best Thing I Ever Did"

I met Sarthak Shukla in a hotel restaurant. Sarthak told me how, as a boy growing up in India, he and his friends bullied a classmate—he said, "It was the usual stuff, we beat him up, called him names, we were relentless."

He explained, "I'm now in my twenties—but my bullying behaviour has continued to haunt me. So on my last trip back to India I took an 800 mile train trip and found this boy—of course, he's now a man. As it turned out, I arrived on the eve of his wedding.

"It was a tearful reunion. I apologized for making his life a misery. I tried to explain that I was the one with the problem, not him. For him, starting a new life as a married man, I know my visit meant a lot.

And for me? It is the best thing I ever did."

# Loneliness Amongst Our Teens

## 10

*Kids aren't born bullies. Bullying is a learned behaviour.*

### You're Black!

I heard an African-American author speaking about her childhood. She said, "When I was six, my best friend was Amy, a little white girl. On our way home from school one day, we stopped at her house.

I asked her, "Can I come inside and play?"

Amy said, "Mommy says, 'No, you can't'."

I asked, "Why not?"

Amy replied, "Mommy says 'No' because you are black!"

Nothing so unusual here—but here's what got my attention. She explained, "That was the first time I realised I was black. Until I was six, I didn't know I was black."

Children are very accepting. They aren't born racist! They learn it. Likewise, kids aren't born bullies. They learn to be bullies.

### In a Nutshell
If bullying is learned, it can be unlearned.

## Growing Up Alone

Last month I noticed a group of eleven-year-olds having a birthday party at our local Italian restaurant. Each kid was playing on his own little computer game, except for one—and he was playing games on his phone. A dozen kids all together and celebrating alone. What kind of a party is that?

In the last 50 years so much has gotten faster, better, more convenient. But some of the convenience isn't helping our kids to be confident, considerate or happy.

We humans evolved as social creatures. We are happiest when we help each other and when we depend on each other.

Until the mid 1900s—even in Western societies—most children lived in homes that bustled with people. Most homes had:

- between three and ten children
- up to five kids crammed into a bedroom
- two parents in the home, plus
- grandparents!

Most often:

- the family ate together, and
- the family made music together, played games together—and until the 1960s, gathered around a single radio or TV.

Children were surrounded by other people. In fact, you couldn't get away from people—brothers, sisters, grandparents.

Compare yesterday's typical family with today's:

- average of about 1.3 children
- kids have their own bedroom, computer, TV—and often, their own bathroom
- a quarter of homes have only one parent
- parents work longer hours and do more shift-work

- everyone eats at different times
- the grandparents have moved out.

In two generations it all changed—homes that bustled with eight or ten people became homes where many children grow up almost alone.

What does this have to do with bullying?

When your little house is full of brothers, sisters and grandparents, you can't help but discuss, play, argue and fight with your family. That's how you refine social skills and sharing skills. That's how children learn, "I am not the centre of the universe and I can't always get what I want."

The answer to the question, "Why the explosion in bullying?" is partly here.

Being with real live people keeps your feet on the ground. To grow up happy and considerate, kids need more than cyber-friends and virtual reality.

## Video Games and Movies

In a scene from the video game, Modern Warfare 2, the players walk calmly into a domestic airport, methodically killing innocent people with automatic weapons. Norwegian mass killer, Anders Breivik, wrote in one of his blogs, "I see Modern Warfare 2 more as part of my training simulation than anything else".

On July 22, 2011, Breivik caught a boat to the little island of Utoya, the venue for a Labour party youth camp. There he walked calmly amongst innocent teenagers, methodically killing 69 of them with automatic weapons.

Here's what we know:

- A mass killer recommends violent video games as an ideal training tool to develop the skills and mindset to inflict tragedy on innocent people.
- Recently 112 academics and professionals from around the world signed a statement affirming a link between violent video games and violent behaviour in even normal individuals.
- The American Academy of Paediatrics reports: "More than a thousand scientific studies and reviews conclude that significant exposure to media violence increases the risk of aggressive behaviour in certain children, desensitises them to violence and makes them believe that the world is a meaner and scarier place than it is."

Here's what my friend, Doug, discovered without the aid of 1000 scientific studies. He tells me, "The longer my son Pat plays video games, the less he

> **His personality changes. I pull him off the computer for a few days and he returns to normal.**

talks to us, the less he wants to help around the house. His personality changes. I pull him off the computer for a few days and he returns to normal."

Of course, the video game industry insists that there is no danger in exposing your child to daily video violence. Would you trust an industry spokesperson or 1000 scientific studies?

### No Damage?

Some parents say, "I let my kids play lots of violent video games—there is no proof it does any damage."

Imagine for a moment there is no proof.

Here's the real question for any parent: Do you raise happy, confident children by asking, "What will do them NO DAMAGE?" Or do you raise happy, confident children by asking, "What will HELP them blossom?" These are two totally different questions.

Let's say your son Charlie plays violent video games for 20 hours a week. Wouldn't he be better off if he spent five hours with his friends, five hours with a guitar or a soccer ball, five hours eating dinner with his family and just five hours chopping off people's heads?

---

**In a Nutshell**

You raise happy, confident children by asking yourself, "What will help them THRIVE?"

---

### What Do You Do?

Three simple steps can help your children:

- Find out about a game before you buy it for your kids—borrow it from a library or DVD store, ask other parents.
- Play video games with your children—then at least you spend time with them and you know what games they are playing. If a game or movie is rated "Parental Guidance", it means you watch it with them.
- Set time limits: "Johnny, you can play for one hour."

# Raising Young Children

## 11

## It's Not Your Kids' Fault

In his book "The Epidemic" here's what psychiatrist and director of the Family Institute of Berkeley, Dr Robert Shaw says about raising kids:

Far too many children today are sullen, unfriendly, distant, preoccupied, and even unpleasant. They whine, nag, throw tantrums, and demand constant attention from their parents, who are spread too thin to spend enough time with them. Feeling guilty and anxious, the parents in turn soothe their kids with unhealthy snacks, faddish clothing, toys, and media...

A host of new 'clinical diagnoses' have been invented to explain why children seem totally spoiled, untrained, and unsocialised, and an incredibly large number of children have been diagnosed with Attention Deficit Hyperactivity Disorder (ADHD) and bombarded with psychoactive drugs...

...we used to be clearer about the importance of parenting, but somehow we've forgotten what children actually require in order to grow into happy, responsible adults. We've lost our sense of what matters most in our children's lives—and when we do know, we're not spending the time and energy to make it happen...

...our stricken children spend much of their time pursuing entertainment rather than accomplishment: TV, video games, mall roaming, computer hacking, substance abuse, [and] promiscuous sex...[9]

Shaw's message to parents is:
- act like grown-ups
- give your children chores and responsibilities
- limit their TV and video game time
- limit their privacy
- teach your children about right and wrong

- don't buy them everything they want, and
- try giving your children love and discipline before you give them drugs.

Shaw has another piece of advice, "…at least one of the parents has to make raising the children the top priority. If you do not, you and your child will live with the consequences the rest of your lives."

*"Stephen's had enough to eat–haven't you Stephen?"*

## Kids Imitate

***"What You Do Speaks So Loudly I Cannot Hear What You Say."***
**Ralph Waldo Emerson**

Did you ever see a two-year-old standing with his hands on his hips, just like his father. Did you ever see a four-year-old scolding the family dog, "Rover! Naughty boy! How many times do I have to tell you?", sounding just like her mother.

How do kids learn this? Does anyone teach them to talk like adults? No. They learn by watching. Psychologists call it MODELLING. It is really just imitation.

Children are like sponges. They copy. Toddlers study their parents—they walk like their parents and talk like their parents. It may be conscious, or unconscious—or a bit of both.

So what happens when a three-year-old watches his father shout at his mother? He learns to shout. What happens when an eight-year-old gets bullied by his older brother? He bullies his younger brother. Not in all cases—but it's common.

Recent discoveries in brain science seem to explain how this happens. In the 1990s Italian scientists observed certain brain cells in macaque monkeys they called mirror neurons. They discovered that when a monkey observes another monkey doing something, the SAME mirror neurons fire as when he does it himself. In other words, the same brain cells are activated—or programmed—when he watches his mother pick up a banana as when he picks up his own banana.

Neuroscientists suggest it is the same for us. Observing behaviour trains your brain. We are programmed to imitate.

Hearing your mother shout programs your mirror neurons—and you learn to shout. Just watching your Dad thump your brother programs you to thump your brother. Just watching your mother comfort a sick friend programs you to be kind.

**In a Nutshell**
Science confirms what we always knew: we learn by example.

## Get Serious!

I watched a mother in an airport warning her five-year-old, "Jack! If you hit Thomas I'll take away your Ipad and you'll never see it again."

Jack hit Thomas and Mum took the Ipad.

As soon as little Jack lost his Ipad, he became an angel. "I'm sorry Thomas, I'm sorry Mummy, I'm so sorry. I won't do it again."

Within three minutes Mum said, "Good boy! Now you have said 'Sorry' you can have your Ipad."

A life sentence without an Ipad was reduced to 180 seconds!

What did Jack learn about hitting Thomas?

- There are no consequences for poor behavior.
- Saying sorry fixes everything.

What did Jack learn about his mother?

- Her threats mean nothing.
- He can get what he wants.

Next time Mum says, "Jack, you must be in bed by seven", Jack will ignore her. He KNOWS she's not really serious. She says stuff but it's just noise.

## Follow Through!

Many people say things but have no intention of following through! Most parents are so used to making idle threats and promises, they don't even realise what is happening.

All the motivators and psychologists say you have to "believe in yourself". That makes sense. But before you can believe in yourself, you have to believe yourself.

When it comes to promises and commitment, so many people are wimps. They say they'll do something, and they don't. They promise they'll help you, and they go fishing. They promise they'll pay their bills, and they leave the country! Then they wonder why their life doesn't work.

How often do parents just go through the motions: they say things but have no intention of following through:

"No, you can't have another ice cream."

"But I want one."

"You've already had two."

"But I'm hungry."

"No."

"Johnny had three!"

"I said 'NO' and THAT'S FINAL"

"Freddy had four."

"I said 'No' and I mean it."

"I want one."

"No."

"I hate you".

"Okay but only this once."

And the worst is yet to come.

Children want to see strength. When you are weak, they keep testing you. But they don't test you because they want to win. They push the boundaries as part of normal childhood development. It is a positive sign. How you respond is what matters.

Kids want strong boundaries. Your three-year-old is saying to himself, "C'mon Mum. Quit being so pathetic! Show some backbone. Make a stand! I want a mother who can follow through!"

> **In a Nutshell**
> Only commit to something if you know you will follow through. If necessary, make less promises and fewer commitments, but whatever *you say you'll do, do it*. Gradually your word becomes law for you—and that's when you really believe in yourself. And that's when people—and your children—begin to show you some respect.

## Little Children Can Be Responsible!

Is this typical? Mum says to her child, "Nick, pick up your toys!" And five minutes later, "Pick up your toys." And five minutes later, "Pick up your toys NOW!" And later, "Nick, pick up your toys or there will be no TV."

The kid continues watching TV and mum picks up the toys. For most parents this is a daily ritual. Why?

A three-year-old that has the skills to eat an ice cream, switch on the TV or ride a scooter, is perfectly capable of collecting Buzz Lightyear and dropping him in a toy box!

Picking up toys is so simple even a child can do it! And some do.

## "Take Care of Your Stuff"

**MARYJANE'S STORY**: When our youngest two children were around three years old they were like any kids—they left their toys wherever they finished with them. We would say, "Pick up your toys." They would ignore us.

So I sat them down and explained very clearly, "You need to take care of your toys. This means you put them back in the toy box when you have finished with them. If you don't look after your toys we will put them in a bag and give them to some poor children who will look after them. "

"Do you understand that if you don't pick up your toys, we will give your toys to poor children?"

"Yes we understand."

That afternoon Julian left his toy train in the lounge room. I asked him to put it away, but he took no notice. It was a beautiful train—a present from his grandmother. So I called Julian, we put it in a bag—and I drove Julian to the charity depot and he left his train for the poor children.

That same week, Vanessa left her beautiful doll in the hallway. I said, "Vanessa, put your dolly away." But she didn't. It was a Christmas present from Uncle Tom, it was Vanessa's favourite dolly. We put the doll in a bag and drove to the depot— and we left Dolly for the poor kids. It broke my heart.

Within a week we had two preschoolers who picked up their toys. There was no shouting, no screaming. They learned to take care of their stuff.

Now they are teenagers and they still take care of their things. Our kids aren't perfect but their rooms are tidy.

My husband Carlo and I made the decision early—we would rather go through a week of pain teaching our children to pick up their toys—than spend the next 12 years arguing with them.

Our children respect us—and they know we follow through.

Children who understand that there are consequences in life are happier—and less likely to create trouble.

How is this connected to bullying? When you have respect for other people, and respect for your things, you are not inclined to punch people and smash things.

## Manners

For thousands of years children have been taught to respect older people. Respect means:

- Greeting your parents when you get up in the morning: "Good morning, Mum".
- Greeting your uncle when he arrives at your house: "Hi Uncle Harry!"
- Greeting your neighbour in the street: "Hello Mr Erwin."
- Saying "please" when you want something.
- Saying "thank you" when somebody gives you a ride to school, a chocolate or twenty dollars.

It is not hard.

For thousands of years, children have learned manners. They learned to acknowledge people, they learned consideration, they learned to make others welcome. In the process children learned that they weren't the centre of the universe.

But the centre of the universe seems to have moved.

These days you can walk into homes where seven-year-old Sally will ignore you completely—or dismiss you with a sideways glance like you're a piece of dog turd. It's not Sally's fault that she has no manners—it's her parents' fault.

Having no manners already puts Sally at a big disadvantage. Why?

Because you don't teach Sally manners for Uncle Harry's benefit. You do it for Sally.

When Sally has manners, people want to talk to her. So Sally feels liked and welcome. She feels a bit special.

When Sally feels special—and liked—she is happier and she doesn't need to bully other kids to try to feel good.

When Sally has manners, Sally's teachers will appreciate her, Sally's friend's parents will welcome her in their home. She'll perform better at job interviews. She might even get a job—so maybe you won't be supporting her when she is 40! Aren't manners wonderful?

Other useful things that children should learn include:

- Running through restaurants and crawling under tables is not acceptable. It shows disrespect for other diners.
- Screaming on the floor of the supermarket until you get an ice cream is not acceptable—and will not be rewarded with an ice cream.
- Playing your music so loud that it keeps the neighbours awake is not cool. It is selfish and inconsiderate.

**In a Nutshell**

Manners lead to respect. When you respect people you don't bully them.

## How Do You Create a Bully?

What encourages kids to misbehave—and bully? When they know, "Whatever I do, I can get away with it."

When your child knows, "My parents make lots of threats but they never follow though," you are headed for trouble. "My parents never follow through" means "I can lie, I can ignore my parents, I can smash things, I can punch other kids and nothing will happen."

Bullying is not about anger. It's about a lack of respect. Bullies bully because they don't care and because they can.

Dan Olweus, professor of psychology at Bergen University, finds four factors that help to create bullies:

- LACK OF WARMTH, LACK OF INVOLVEMENT from the parents, particularly the mother.
- NO CLEAR LIMITS on aggressive behaviour. If the child is allowed to hit and bully his brothers and neighbours, he will become more and more aggressive.
- PHYSICAL PUNISHMENT. Children that are disciplined with violence learn violence.
- THE TEMPERAMENT OF THE CHILD. Hot-headed children are more likely to become bullies.

## Empathy: How Kids Learn It

Empathy is appreciating how others feel. But if a child doesn't know what she feels, she has no way to understand how another child feels.

Here's a typical scenario: Mum walks into the lounge room to find three-year-old Mary kicking little brother Eric.

Mum says, "You apologise to your brother NOW!"

Mary says, "Sorry, Eric."

Mum says, "You go to your room until I tell you to come out." Mary goes to her room sobbing. Twenty minutes later she is released. Mary learns that there are consequences when she kicks Eric, but little else.

Many parents in this situation will simply say, "I'm angry with you!" This doesn't help much.

Children don't automatically see things from another child's point of view.

Mary needs Mum to explain things a little, "I know you were upset, Mary. When you kicked your brother, that hurt him."

For Mary to quit kicking people, Mary also needs to discover more about being angry, being jealous, being happy and sad.

### Feelings into Words

Learning to put words to things helps children to understand. For example, you explain Mary's world to her by giving her words, "This is a bear", "This is a duck".

Once she has labels for things Mary can ask you questions, "Why does the duck have funny feet?" Once she has names for things she is better able to ask herself questions. "Why don't bears have beaks?" Having words to describe things helps children ponder.

So how do you help Mary understand emotions? By teaching her words for different emotions.

After Mary has finished kicking Eric, and when she has been released from her bedroom and everyone has calmed down, you talk with her about feelings.

"Why did you kick Eric?"

"Eric threw my bear in the toilet"

"Well Mary, how do you feel about that?"

"How would you feel if Eric kicked you?"

At other times you might discuss characters in Mary's storybooks, and encourage her to give names to their feelings: "Look at Billy's face. How does he feel?" You teach her about feelings by asking: "Where in your body do you feel happy, sad, angry?" And you help her to imagine: "How would you feel, Mary, if you lost Snoopy?"

As Mary learns to describe how she feels, she becomes less frustrated. She will probably kick Eric less often.

Teaching children about feelings might not appear to be critical—but it is

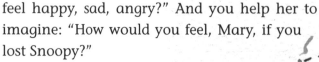

directly related to bullying. Here's why:

- When you can put your feelings into words, you are happier. Happy children—and adults—are less inclined to make other people suffer.
- Empathy—or appreciating how other people feel—happens in two stages:
  1. we learn to give words to how we feel. Once we know how WE feel,
  2. we begin to appreciate how OTHER PEOPLE feel.

When you appreciate how others feel, you don't bully other people. You don't kick them in the head, you don't steal their lunch money or send text messages that say, "I'm going to kill you".

Your four-year-old can only feel empathy if he feels okay about himself. If he is hurting, lonely, feeling stupid or unloved, there is no room to worry about anyone else's feelings.

Most bullies were never encouraged to explore their own feelings—or were bullied themselves. For example, when parents bully children they say things like:

- "Do what I say or I'll belt you."
- "Stop crying or I'll give you something to cry about!"
- "I'm not interested in your story."
- "I wish you were never born."
- "I'm going to send you to the orphanage!"

None of the above encourages an exploration of feelings.

A dog senses when you're in pain. Elephants and dolphins are empathetic. Almost any child can feel empathy.

In a nursery—when one baby cries, another will cry. After a year or so, children learn that they are individuals. A toddler will try to soothe a crying baby. But empathy needs to be nurtured.

**In a Nutshell**
Happy, well-adjusted children don't enjoy seeing other kids cry.

**Teach by Example**

If you say to your four-year-old daughter, "Johnny looks very sad. He has no friends to play with!", she can understand. Tell her, "Poor Johnny wakes up every day hoping that he will make a friend. But he walks to school alone, he spends his lunch hour alone, kids make fun of his glasses and his skinny legs. He cries himself to sleep every night." A four-year-old can feel sad.

If you ask her, "What could you do to make him feel better?" She'll respond.

If you explain to a young child, "Timmy's Mummy and Daddy don't have a job so they don't have much money. They can't afford nice clothes like you have. How would you feel if you had no nice clothes?" A child can understand.

### In a Nutshell
Children are kind when they are encouraged to be kind.

## Make Children Responsible

Children who learn responsibility also learn caring. It's part of the same deal— feed the cat, take out the garbage, tidy your room. The child learns, "What I do matters, what I do affects my world".

You teach them how to care by showing you care.

When you help others, involve your children. You help a neighbour change a light bulb, you give clothes to the local charity, do it together. Talk to them about poor people. Take a drive to poor neighbourhoods.

Despite what we might believe, little boys can be as caring as little girls. They just need to be encouraged.

And here's more good news. Educationalists tell us that caring children become better students and more successful people. Why? Because it takes imagination and flexible thinking to appreciate how somebody else feels. Empathy stretches your brain.

### In a Nutshell
We are born with the seeds of empathy—but it needs to be nurtured. You cannot feel empathy AND bully someone.

## Discipline: Four Keys

There seem to be four essentials in teaching children to be respectful and responsible.

1. TALK YOUR CHILD'S LANGUAGE What does he value most? If Billy's favourite toy is his tricycle, then that is what you take away when he kicks his sister. When you talk tricycle, you have his attention!

2. PREDICTABLE CONSEQUENCES. Billy needs to know ahead of time: If I do A, I get B. Billy knows, "If I kick my little sister, I lose my tricycle—any time, any day of the week same punishment." When the outcome is predictable, three things happen:
   - Billy realises that his parents are fair
   - Billy begins to understand causes and consequences
   - Billy realises that he is actually in control: I do A, I get B.

3. DON'T TAKE IT PERSONALLY. Avoid comments like, "I am so disappointed in you." Instead, "You understand that because you did A you now get B". Discipline without anger and without endless warnings.
   Be caring and firm. The foundation of effective punishment is: "I love you. Your behaviour is not acceptable."

4. FOLLOW THROUGH. You MUST deliver!

## Discipline in Action

First let's agree that SOME THINGS ARE A CHILD'S RIGHT. Your child has a right to a warm bed. Your child has a right to have enough to eat. No matter how she behaves, it is not fair to send her to bed hungry. It's cruel. How would you like to go to bed hungry?

THERE ARE ALSO PRIVILEGES: television, video games, parties, shopping, excursions, concerts, sports games etc.

So let's look at how you can incorporate the Four Keys of Discipline:

STEP 1: Get a whiteboard and hang it in the kitchen or the family room. Make a list of all Billy's privileges.

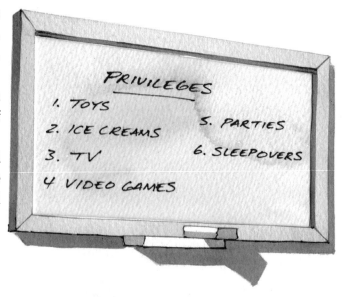

PRIVILEGES
1. TOYS
2. ICE CREAMS
3. TV
4. VIDEO GAMES
5. PARTIES
6. SLEEPOVERS

STEP 2:

You establish some house rules, for example:

- No hitting each other
- No name-calling
- No screaming or whining
- Finish your homework on time

STEP 3: You explain to Billy, "When you obey the house rules we have a happy home. If you break a house rule, you will lose privilege #1. If you break another rule, you will lose privilege no #2—as well as privilege #1.

When you obey house rules for 3 days you get back privilege #2, obey house rules for another 3 days you get back privilege #1. (For older children you might like to use intervals of 1 week).

What's good about this system?

- Billy knows where he stands.
- You know where you stand. You don't have to invent penalties on the spot. You don't have to get angry. No need for discussion or arguments. You don't have to give endless warnings and threats.

Note: This system is explained by Stan Davis at www.stopbullyingnow.com.

Healthy kids will push boundaries and ask for things. Healthy kids will sometimes try to control other children. Just because a young child tries to get his own way doesn't mean he is going to become a bully. What's important is how you deal with it.

# Who's in Charge?

## 12

## The Rocket

When I was in high school we had a geography teacher called Mr Roberts. Mr Roberts—we called him "Rocket"—was a gentle, decent man who expected to treat us as civilised equals.

But we weren't his equals and we weren't civilised. We were thirteen!

*"When I was a teenager, I was proud to be seen with my parents!"*

Mr Roberts knew a lot about geography but he had no idea how to control teenagers. So we would test him. We talked throughout his lectures, we launched paper aeroplanes, we laid on the floor and lit cigarettes. I drew rude cartoons on the blackboard. We made his life hell. Yet, we weren't a bad bunch of kids—and we liked him. So why?

We were thirteen-year-olds. When you are thirteen, it is frightening to be in the hands of an adult who is unsure of himself. So you test him, hoping that he will draw the line. We wanted Mr Roberts to take control—and so we pushed and pushed. Within a year he left.

But WE didn't want to win. We wanted some boundaries.

Your children are the same.

When your three-year-old senses that you are uncertain or out of control, she becomes confused and frightened. So she kicks and screams and makes ridiculous demands. She is hoping that, unlike Rocket Roberts, you will calmly take control.

Here's what your children DON'T WANT:

- they don't want you to take instructions from them
- they don't want you to plead with them to behave
- they don't want you to shout and scream
- they don't want you to hover around asking endless questions: "Do you want this, do you want that, do you want another drink...?"

And they don't want you to apologise endlessly! Where did THAT come from? So many parents are now in permanent apology mode. Just recently, Julie and I saw a four-year-old screaming at his mother from the back seat of a car, "You say sorry! You say sorry NOW!" Obviously the kid is used to apologies and felt he was due for another.

When your child is three, there is a lot that needs to be explained: this is a cow, this is a rooster ..." There is also a lot that doesn't need to be explained, eg:

- "You are going to bed now." No explanation necessary.
- "No more ice cream." No explanation necessary.
- "Don't set fire to Daddy's trousers." No explanation necessary.

So what do children WANT?

> **66** *Children want you to set rules and stick by them.* **99**

- They want you to be firm and calm.
- They want you to be consistent.
- They want you to set rules and stick by them.
- They want you to be around.

## Who is Making the Decisions?

Some parents treat their kids like friends. Your ten-year-old doesn't need you to be a friend. He can find those at school. What he needs is a parent.

Some parents let kids make decisions that are parents' decisions: nine-year-old Bianca is having a tantrum. Mum says, "So where do you want to go next vacation— do you want to go sailing or do you want to go to the snow?"

Bianca is kicking the furniture. She doesn't want sun or snow. Mum is pleading, trying to make her happy, "Well, where do you want to go?"

WHAT? Since when does a nine-year-old decide how to spend the family savings?

Sure, you can discuss options. Talk about going to the moon if you like. But then YOU MAKE THE DECISION and you tell Bianca, "We are going to Uncle Ted's farm".

How often do you see Mums in the kitchen taking dinner orders from five-year-olds like the kid is a princess and Mum is the waitress: "Would you like chicken or fish? And would you like fries with that?

Next day Dad says to the five-year-old, "We're eating out. Do you want to eat Chinese or Italian?"

Since when does a five-year-old run the house? As kids become teenagers, sure you involve them in discussions about where they want to go on vacation and where they want to eat. But not five-year-olds!

In some families, negotiating is the in-thing. You don't negotiate with a five-year-old! You negotiate with your bank manager.

When kids are five, they can make some decisions: "Today I'll wear my green shirt". Other things you TELL them, "This is what we are eating tonight, this is where we are going tomorrow." A five-year-old is very comfortable and secure with that. A five-year-old is happy with that.

> 66 *You don't negotiate with a five-year-old! You negotiate with your bank manager.* 99

Sometimes your teenagers will ask you, "How come you get to make the rules? How come you get to make the decisions?" You explain, "Because I am your parent and I pay the bills. When you are a parent and you pay the bills, you get to make the rules." End of story.

### "I'm Sorry"

In some families, "Sorry" is the magic word that excuses kids from all bad behaviour. The kids know, "I can be as mean and nasty as I like—and then I just say, 'Sorry'. The kids know, "I can be careless and reckless and then protest, 'It was an accident!'"

Is sorry enough?

> 66 *I can be as mean and nasty as I like—and then I just say, 'Sorry'.* 99

Imagine this: you are driving past your neighbour Jim's house when you spill a steaming cappuccino into your lap. Your groin is on fire! In the excitement of the moment you accelerate off the road, through Jim's rose garden and into his lounge room.

When the dust settles, you crawl out of your car window to find Jim wedged between your bumper and his flat-screen TV. Jim now has a fractured pelvis, two broken legs and a large hole in his house.

You say, "Sorry Jim, it was an accident."

Saying "sorry" would be enough, right? You didn't mean to demolish his home and put him in hospital. You meant no harm. Would sorry be enough?

NO! NO! NO! You are responsible. Accident or not, you are accountable. You need to pay to repair Jim and his house. And you will likely be charged with a traffic offence and fined for driving without due care.

There are laws—fair and consistent penalties—to punish people who hurt others. If you are penalised by the law it doesn't necessarily mean you are a criminal. But fair consequences encourage us to be considerate and responsible.

It is the same for two-year-olds and sixteen-year-olds who cause hurt. Fair and consistent penalties encourage them to be considerate and responsible. It's not enough for a child to say, "Sorry" or "It was an accident".

In his book *Empowering Bystanders in Bullying Prevention*, Stan Davis writes: "We help young people when we hold them accountable, regardless of their intent. Many young people believe that by stating that they intended no harm, they can avoid responsibility for their actions. The truth in most situations is that harm is done and is the result of a choice." [10]

Kids need to be accountable—and behave.

**In a Nutshell**
I'm sorry doesn't mean it is over.

## "Mum Will Take Care of It"

Mum gave fourteen-year-old Amelia her first phone. Mum explained, "This phone is for emergencies and brief calls. You are allowed to use $100 per month."

Next month Amelia got her first phone bill: it was $1,100! Mum went crazy. Amelia blamed the phone company. So Mum called and abused the phone company who agreed to slash the bill by half. Mum paid the $550.

What did Amelia learn?

Next month Amelia's bill was $1,358. Mum went crazy. Amelia blamed the phone company. The phone company wouldn't budge. Mum paid the $1358. What has Amelia learned? What has Mum learned?

What should Mum do now? What she should have done two months ago. Take the phone away or put a limit on the phone!

## Dad Will Take Care of It

The December that Mick turned 16, his parents gave him a shiny Mazda. Mick was very happy.

- The following January, Mick was speeding down a country road and tried to overtake a truck and trailer on a blind corner. Too late he saw the oncoming car. Mick swerved in front of the truck, the truck driver hit the brakes and the trailer hit a tree. Miraculously no one was hurt. The truck driver, who had a wife and three children, had no truck and no work for three weeks. Mick's dad paid to repair the Mazda. What did Mick learn? Nothing, except *Dad will take care of it.*

- In March: Mick got a speeding ticket. Mick couldn't pay the two hundred dollars. Mick didn't have the money. Dad paid it. And Mick learned? Nothing, except *Dad will take care of it.*

- In June: Mick got arrested for underage drink-driving. Mick, his mother and father attended court. Dad hired a smart lawyer, Dad paid the fine and Mick was back on the road. What did Mick learn? Nothing, except *Dad will take care of it.*

- In September: Mick rolled the Mazda into a ditch—it was completely wrecked so Dad bought him a Toyota. Mick was back on the road within three weeks. What did Mick learn? Nothing, except *Dad will take care of it.*

- At 18 Mick wrecked the Toyota—he was traveling too fast and hit a tree. Dad bought Mick a big red Ford V8 and Mick was back on the road.

By now no insurance company in the country wanted anything to do with Mick. It took Dad a few dozen phone calls and a lot of fast talking—but finally, Dad got a policy for Mick and his Ford. What did Mick learn? Nothing, except *Dad will take care of it.*

- At 19, with a red V8 and a new insurance company, Mick tried to pass a truck at high speed—without signaling. As Mick swerved right, so did the truck. Mick's car went under the truck. The impact tore off the entire roof of his car. The police later explained, "It was like a lid ripped off a sardine can." Mick suffered serious brain damage and can't speak. He is semi-paralysed down his entire right side. He lost half his sight.

Mick will never drive again. Dad will be taking care of Mick for the rest of his life. Mick's life—and the life of his whole family—changed in an instant.

## "He's Learned His Lesson"

My friend Alex has an eighteen-year-old son, Ben. Ben has had the best of everything—schools, coaching, cars, overseas trips. Alex would do anything for Ben—and maybe that is the problem.

Six months ago Alex told me, "Ben got arrested last night. He thumped someone outside a nightclub and the police locked him up. It cost me $1800 to get him out! Ben is a real headache—mixing with the wrong crowd. I don't know what to do with him."

I said, "Why did YOU pay it?"

He said, "Ben hasn't got any money. Hopefully he's learned his lesson."

Last month I bumped into Alex and he told me, "Ben got arrested last night. He was caught urinating in a park—and then he thumped a policeman. They put him in a cell. It cost me $2000 to get him out!"

I said, "Why did YOU pay it?" Alex seemed annoyed by my question.

He said, "Ben hasn't got any money. I think he's learned his lesson."

This month? Ben was arrested for selling drugs on the street.

What has Ben learned?

## Parents Helping Out

When you do everything for you child, does he respect you any more? Does he love you any more? Does he take responsibility?

Being the nice guy is the easy way out. When Dad says, "I'm doing this for my son", the reality may be, "I want to be the good guy, I want to be Mr Fixit." The truth may be, "I want to be his friend."

While you protect your child from consequences, the consequences keep getting bigger.

Teenagers are like anybody. They learn from small doses of pain, inconvenience and disappointment. It is called real life.

### In a Nutshell
Life is always nudging us with signals. When we ignore the signals, we get a sledgehammer.

## The Teenage Brain

*"The teenage brain is not just an adult brain with fewer miles on it,"*
**Frances E. Jensen, Professor of Neurology.**

Seventeen-year-old Kevin is intelligent, loving and respectful—he is an A student with a bright future. One Saturday night he hit the town with his mates and they all got drunk.

The guys spotted their teacher's car parked in an alley. One said, "Hey, just for a laugh, let's steal his hubcaps!"

At that moment, just by chance, a police car drove by. The boys sprinted into the bushes and Kevin was left holding the hubcaps. He was arrested and charged.

Isn't it a typical story? Why do intelligent teenagers do stupid things?

Research since 2000 has surprised the medical community. Scientists now tell us that the brain of a teenager is only 80% developed. The frontal lobe of the cortex doesn't fully connect to the rest of the brain until somewhere between ages 25 and 30.

You say, so what?

Here's what: the frontal lobe of the cortex handles REASONING, PLANNING, and JUDGEMENT. There's a reason why teenagers do crazy things! There's a reason why teenagers are impulsive, there's a reason why they sometimes drive fast and take risks. There's a reason why they care so much about what their friends think.

Teens aren't wired to think of long-term consequences. Mary breaks up with Toby—she thinks it's the end! Dave fails an exam and wants to quit school.

We think that because a fifteen-year-old is bigger than his dad, he should think like an adult. But he doesn't—and he can't.

### In a Nutshell
Teenagers have powerful brains but they are still learning to drive them.

### Teen Sex
When my wife Julie and I were researching our book, *Being a Happy Teen*, we were invited to dinner at a neighbour's home.

There were three couples at the dinner including Julie and me—plus three young girls. Our neighbours' girl, Karen, was thirteen. The other couple had the two girls—one fourteen and the other twelve. The three teens were bright and confident—and all good students. Both couples were obviously proud and caring parents.

When dinner was over, the teenagers went inside to watch TV—and our conversation turned to teenage sex. Karen's dad said, "I know Karen has never had sex. She wouldn't dare!" His wife agreed.

The other father said, "I know Melanie and Rachel have never had sex". His wife added, "We know where they go and who they mix with!"

Later in the evening Julie went inside to join the three girls. They chatted about school, fashion and boys. Out of curiosity, Julie asked the girls, "What is a good age to start having sex?"

Thirteen-year-old Karen said: "Sixteen".

Fourteen-year-old Melanie said: "Sixteen".

Rachel, the youngest, said: "Yeah, I think sixteen..."

Julie asked: "Why not earlier?"

Melanie suggested: "Because you're not ready for it?"

The other two agreed: "Not before sixteen."

So then Julie asked: "So, have any of you had sex?"

Melanie: "I have".

Karen: "I have".

Twelve-year-old Rachel said: "Not real sex—only oral sex."

Julie asked: "Where did you do it?"

And the answer for each of them was: "At home". Melanie added, "Where else? I haven't got a car!"

Julie asked: "Were your parents home at the time?"

And the answer for each girl was: "Yes they were!"

Parents think they know what is going on—and they don't have a clue. The saddest part of all—none of the girls wanted to have sex. Each of them felt pressured into it by boyfriends.

Julie asked them, "Did you enjoy it?"

Two said, "Not at all." One said, "It was awful".

So why did you do it? "Because all the girls do it."

*"I know my husband can be loving and kind—*
*he's that way with the dog!"*

# Let Your Children Know You Love Them

## 13

**VICKI'S STORY:** I come from an Asian country. My mother sent me out to work as a maid when I was ten. My bosses didn't treat me very well. I never went to school. My life was horrible.

Anyway, I came to Australia, met Dave, fell in love and got married. We both had no money. We worked hard and long hours so we could buy our own little house and eventually have a family.

Dave drove a taxi and I cleaned houses and toilets. I still clean houses and toilets because I have no qualifications. I had no education.

We have two children, Jessica and Tim. I swore that my children would have a better life than I had. I promised myself that they would have a proper education and a normal life like other Australian kids. I swore that they would never have to clean filthy toilets for a living like me—that they would enjoy the toys I never had, and have the clothes I never had.

We needed a second car so I got a second job stacking supermarket shelves at night. Often I would get home from the supermarket at 3am. I was too tired to get up and see my kids off to school, so they walked themselves to school.

I was working so hard that I was too tired to cook. We lived on take-away hamburgers and pizzas. To earn more money I got a third job ironing on weekends.

Jessica is now seventeen. She used to complain that she never saw me but I had to work. We needed the money. I tried staying home some nights, but even when I was home the kids just watched TV. If my kids don't talk to me, what is the point of being at home? I might as well be stacking shelves at the supermarket.

Jessica dropped out of school last year and moved out.

My son Tim is now sixteen. When Tim was ten he started getting into trouble for bullying at school. He was punching other boys in the playground. He was also picked up by the police for throwing bricks through the neighbours' windows. Tim is a good boy, really. He just started hanging out with the wrong crowd.

> **"** *Tim's teachers labelled him a problem child. But the teachers picked on him for no reason.* **"**

Tim's teachers labelled him a problem child. But the teachers picked on him for no reason. So we pulled Tim out of that school and enrolled him in an expensive private school, hoping the new school could discipline him.

We couldn't really afford the fees but we were desperate for him to get some help. I began working longer hours to pay extra school fees! We hoped the new school would teach him some values. But Tim continued to bully kids and get into trouble. I was constantly being called to the new school regarding Tim's bullying.

It was all too much for my husband. He got real stressed and started drinking.

By fifteen Tim had a drug habit. He got suspended from the new school for bullying and bad behaviour. The school recommended counselling and rehabilitation which cost us thousands.

We raised the money by renting Jessica's room to a Korean student. Tim resented having a stranger in the house. He would lose his temper. He got more angry and out of control.

Tim kept telling us, "I hate you, I hate school, I hate everything!" He dropped out of school and began an apprenticeship as a chef. He liked it for a while and then quit.

Tim's negative attitude got worse and worse and he suffered depression. Lately he's been threatening suicide. So I quit work to stay home with Tim. That's what I do now—stay home to make sure Tim doesn't kill himself.

Both our kids have dropped out of school. We are almost broke. Tim just wants to die. This is not the life my husband and I had planned for our kids.

---

Vicki is a loving and caring Mum. She has always looked after her children the best way she knows how. Every dollar she makes, she spends on her children. She had no mentor. She didn't understand how important it was to spend time with her kids.

Tim now has his mum at home—which is what he wanted ten years ago—but it's ten years too late.

Parents may have the best intentions to create a better life for their kids—but sometimes parents are too close to see what is happening.

Sometimes we tell ourselves that we are doing our best for our kids—but we are actually doing what *is most convenient*. Sometimes, we would rather be at work than at home—and we pretend we are doing it *only for the kids*.

Here's what is generally true:

- For a ten-year-old, *no leather lounge suite, fancy apartment or sparkling new Hyundai* is compensation for not having your parents' time and attention.
- What you don't give your kids—in guidance and discipline—*no school* can replace.
- If your son is troubled and he becomes a bully, changing schools probably won't help.
- Sure, your children want your time and your attention—but sometimes just being in the house is enough reassurance for a child.
- When you are twelve—and your parents are always working—any attention is better than no attention. Smashing windows, getting drunk, bullying the neighbours will usually work—in the beginning. Tim's dad says, "But I don't understand why he does this!" Tim's strategy is simple and very common, "You may not approve of me but at least you will notice me."
- When nobody is at home, any crowd is better than no crowd. Almost any gang is better than absent parents. Everyone wants to belong. If you don't have someone to talk to, if you don't have role models at home, you find support elsewhere. Gangs are a replacement for family. Gangs don't judge.

**In a Nutshell**
Life is a trade-off. What you don't do now, comes back to bite you.

The time you don't spend exercising before sixty years of age you will likely spend in hospitals after sixty. The small credit card bills you don't pay off today can cripple you within a few years.

The time you don't spend with your kids before they are fifteen you will likely spend later in life—worrying about them and trying to repair the damage. It is often too late.

## What Do You Know About Your Children?

Some parents think they know their children—yet they don't know the answers to simple questions like:

- Who are your best friends?
- What do you spend your money on?
- What subjects are you studying?
- Who are your heroes?

You don't get to know your children by spending ten minutes of "quality time" with them each week.

If you are a boss, you might be able to call in a manager for a ten minute meeting; "Just give me the essentials. What's on your mind?"

But being a parent doesn't work the same. If you have a ten minute meeting with your thirteen-year-old they'll tell you nothing. Only when you spend hours and hours of time with them—eat with them, play with them, vacation with them do you discover a little of how they are thinking.

You have to be around, you have to be familiar. When it suits them—and not when it suits you—they will open up.

### In a Nutshell

Teenagers are a bit like wild animals—it takes a lot of time to get their confidence and they are more scared than you are!

## Let Your Kids Know You Care

Julie and I were on a plane to Fiji in 2011. In front of us was a family of four: Mum, Dad, a four-year-old boy and an eight-month-old baby. The four-year-old sat playing quietly with his Nintendo, occasionally glancing at his parents.

Three hours into the trip, Julie nudged me and said, "These adoring parents haven't left their baby alone for a minute. They have rocked him, stroked him, kissed and cuddled him since Sydney—and he was asleep the whole time."

She said, "The baby is asleep. Why do you think the parents don't leave him alone?"

Julie suggested, "Parents don't smother babies with cuddles for the baby's benefit. It's because parents enjoy it. It is so nice to kiss a baby."

Then she asked me, "How many times do you think they have touched, cuddled kissed or even talked to the four-year-old?"

Of course I had no idea but Julie had been watching them for three hours. The answer was, "Hardly at all."

Her point was not that we should cuddle babies less. But that we could cuddle children more. What does a four-year-old—who spent three years being the centre of attention, think when the new baby arrives? "What is the matter with me?"

Of course, kids become more independent as they grow. They don't want to be smothered. But many children go from being thoroughly adored to mostly ignored almost overnight.

Because of how we were raised, some of us find it hard to tell our children we love them. But there are ways. If you have trouble telling your son you love him, leave a message on his bed, put a note in his lunchbox, say it in a birthday card.

Some parents write letters to their children, even while their kids are living in the same house: "Dear Jane, Mum and I are so proud of you. Sometimes we get so busy and stressed that we forget to tell you how much we love you. You mean more to us than you will ever know..."

Would your teenager appreciate a note like that? It doesn't cost much. You don't even have to post it.

## Treat Your Kids Better Than Your Neighbours!

This morning you promised your five-year-old son, Jack, that you would play ball with him. It's now three o'clock. He asks, "When are we going to play ball?"

"In a minute."

"When?"

"Soon."

At four o'clock, he asks, "Dad, can we play ball now?"

"In a minute."

There's a knock on the door and it's your neighbour, Rudy.

"Hey, Rudy! Come on in. Sit down. Have a beer! How's your week? What are you up to? Have some cheese, have some crackers!"

Your boy says, "Dad, when are we going to play ball?"

"Not now", you say. "Can't you see Rudy is here?"

Meanwhile, Rudy has settled in for the evening. He has already demolished the entire cheese platter and he is boring you to death. You think, "I had better be polite. Another beer, Rudy?"

Why all the effort to impress the neighbour? Who do you care most about?

Why do we treat neighbours and friends better than our kids that we love most?

If you made a promise to your boy, keep it. Sometimes you have to say to Rudy, "Not now. I promised Jack I would play with him."

Parents talk to their children like they would never talk to their neighbours! Would Dad lean over the fence and say, "Rudy, you're hopeless. You're stupid! You're an idiot!"? But dads do it to their boys.

It takes seconds to humiliate a child and crush his spirit. Just one, "You're useless!" can do it. It takes a hundred "I love you's" and "I am proud of you's" to build him back up.

## "I Gave the Bullies Respect"

**HELEN'S STORY:** As a child I was regularly bullied at school. One girl, Natalie, hounded me. She criticised my clothes, my shoes, she laughed at how I spoke and scoffed at what I said. This may seem like small stuff—but when you are six-years-old, or ten, and it happens daily—it damages you.

Teachers told me this was normal teasing and it would toughen me up. Natalie chipped away at my self-esteem for six years. I never knew why. I just assumed there was something wrong with me.

Natalie's crusade cast a long shadow over my teen years. Natalie convinced me I was ugly. I became withdrawn and self-critical. I would over-analyse my decisions and beat myself up. It was not until my mid-twenties that I really recovered.

When I became a school teacher (of 11-16 year olds), I was determined to handle whatever bullying I discovered with care and consideration—as I wish it had been dealt with when I was a target in school.

I remember once, a lad called Liam from my tutorial class got into trouble for fighting. He wasn't the kind of boy to get into fights—so I pulled him aside and we had a chat.

It turned out that he was being bullied. A group of seven children were taunting him and making fun of his ginger hair. He told me that his parents had advised him to hit back at anyone who bullied him. Like most kids he was hesitant to tell me the details. But when I assured him everything would be okay, he told me about the students who were calling him names.

## "What Gives You the Right?"

I met with the seven offenders in the corridor. My intent was not to shame them but to see the best in them. I said, "I'm surprised to hear this! You are all decent individuals."

I felt sympathy for the boy and I let them feel my concern. Intent not to judge them and with as much understanding as I could muster, I asked them, "Do you realise that you are bullying this boy?"

I asked them, "What gives you the right to criticise his hair?"

Two of the girls immediately burst into tears. The others became silent and were genuinely sorry. Without any prompting from me, they asked if they could apologise to the lad—and they did so. To the best of my knowledge the bullying never happened again.

Why was the strategy successful? The 'bullies' didn't feel victimised or labeled. They simply needed an understanding adult to reveal how their behaviour was causing hurt to another. They kept their dignity, and so they were much more able to be the good people we all are inside.

## Coping Skills

How different my childhood could have been. No one ever taught me basic skills that would have helped me deal with Natalie:

- You can walk away. Just because someone is abusing you, you don't have to stand there and cop it.
- You don't have to be RIGHT. You don't have to be SEEN TO BE RIGHT. You don't have to stand there and argue.

People say, "Bullying will make her a stronger person". Lots of things make you a stronger person. Cancer will make you a stronger person. Losing your brother in an accident—which also happened to me—will make you a stronger person. But I wouldn't wish such things on anyone.

If one teacher of authority, or if Natalie's father, had stepped in and asked her, "What gives you the right to criticise someone?", how different might things have been?

Helen's email: helenpeuleve@hotmail.co.uk

## Good Kids Make Mistakes

All bullying isn't vicious or premeditated. Sometimes bullying is just kids being kids. Sometimes it's merely thoughtlessness.

Most kids can be sympathetic. With a little encouragement most kids will see another's point of view.

### In a Nutshell
You don't fix every bullying incident with a hammer.

# Praise and Criticism

When you praise people, they usually do two things:

    1. they openly admit that there is more that they could do, and

    2. they try to be better.

When you criticise people, they usually:

    a) defend themselves, and

    b) make no attempt to improve!

And also, they hate you for it!

EXAMPLE: You say to your neighbour, Wendy, "You are a wonderful mother!" She'll say, "I could be better. I make so many mistakes."

But try telling Wendy what she *already knows*, "You could be a much better mother. You make so many mistakes!" What then? She'll probably whack you—or bomb your house!

Similarly, you say to a twelve-year-old bully, "You are a good kid. I can see that you are a kind person." He'll be speechless. He'll reflect on how he could be better. Chances are he'll make an effort to be more like the person you see in him. Chances are he'll remember your comment for the rest of his life.

But try telling the same kid, "You are evil, you are a loser. You have no future." He'll decide, "Why make an effort? People tell me I'm bad, and I probably am."

Shame and punishment aren't the whole solution to bullying. If all you do is shame and embarrass a bully he will decide, "I am a bad person and next time I do this I will make sure I don't get caught!"

**In a Nutshell**
When you see the best in people, they see the best in themselves.

## Two Types of Praise

It is important how we praise. Stan Davis writes:

> We can tell young people they are smart, or tell them that they worked hard. Does it make a difference?
>
> I used to tell kids they were smart, or caring, or talented. Then I found the

research of Dr. Carol Dweck, who found that young people who are praised in this way—for their traits—have a hard time when things go wrong. She found that kids who think: "I did well on that assignment, and that means I'm smart" may feel stupid when they do badly on an assignment. These students would only raise their hands when they were sure they were right, and would stop trying if they got bad grades. I think of the music teacher who told me: "I never tell my students they have a gift for music, because when I do they stop practising!"

On the other hand, when we tell children what we see them doing, we help them realise that learning takes hard work. Instead of saying to themselves: "I'm smart," they say, "I try hard and don't give up." Dweck found that these students keep trying when the work gets harder.

We can say: "You kept practising until you learned to ride your bike!" "You used good table manners at the restaurant." "You got ready for bed on time." "You kept working—and you finished your homework." "You controlled yourself when you had to wait."

This is one of a series of practical newsletters by Stan Davis, author of *Schools Where Everyone Belongs*, available at www.stopbullyingnow.com.

# 14. What You Can Do

## "Bullied All My Life"

**T**ORI MATTHEWS-OSMAN'S STORY:
Sitting on the kitchen floor, I drag the paring knife across my wrist, gradually applying more and more pressure. The blade cuts my skin and I watch the blood trickle. I have hit rock bottom.

I remember little things from my past, things that led to this:

### 2000: Primary School

Age five and starting primary school: it was the year my dad moved out and the time the bullying started. I was quiet and shy. I tried my best in class. Other kids called me "Ugly", "Teacher's Pet", "No Friends". Mum was going through her own hell. I didn't want to worry her more so I kept the bullying from her for the whole year. I always told Mum I was okay. I have never felt more alone than at that point. Mum thought I was just struggling with the upheaval at home.

Mum walked me to school every day. When we got to the school gate, I wouldn't want to let go of Mum's hand, wondering, "What will happen to me today?" I remember throwing tantrums as Mum walked me to class, crying and screaming that I didn't want to be there. The thought of school made me sick. I would be dragged away by a teacher who sat me at the back of the classroom as she pulled out her guitar for "songtime".

### 2003—2006: More Bullying

Primary school was my own personal hell, designed to torture me. I recall the countless times I cried at night, dreading the next day at school, feeling physically sick. I would have headaches and fits of vomiting. I cried as I lay in bed, before getting ready for school, during school, at recess, lunch or in

> **❝** *Primary school was my own personal hell, designed to torture me.* **❞**

the middle of class, and after school.

I did all I could to avoid school, to be free of the bullies and their taunts for just one day: Every day it was, "You're fat", "You're ugly", "Useless bitch!"

I recall how my poor Mum didn't know what to do. She was desperate to get some help for me. Countless times I saw my mum furious that the school was doing nothing—Mum would march into the school and yell at the teachers, "Do something to stop the bullying!" Mum even shouted at the principal, "Do something!"

The teachers promised that they would help—that they would do something, that they would talk to the bullies. Each time I remember the tiny glimmer of hope it gave me. The bullying would stop for a day or two at most—and then it would start all over again.

### 2007—2010: High School

I was so fearful and nervous starting high school. I had no friends there. I had heard that the high school bullies were relentless—and it was true. Now the boys joined the girls with sexual innuendoes, more insults, more humiliation. It became more vicious. Any name you can think of, I've been called it: "Slut", "Hooker", "Prostitute", "Whore".

Boys would make sexual remarks about my breasts, calling them watermelons—and they would try to touch them, and sometimes they did. I felt so humiliated, embarrassed and awful. I wondered if I was some kind of freak.

I think of the threats on Facebook: "I'm gonna hit you!", "Watch your back!" I remember trying to avoid the bullies at lunchtime. I was so scared, eating my sandwiches alone in a toilet cubicle, hiding until classes started.

As I'm cutting at my wrist I can't help the thoughts running through my mind. "Maybe they're right!" "Perhaps I am useless, stupid, good for nothing, a waste of space. I am hideous, aren't I? I am fat and ugly; who would ever want me?"

A tidal wave of hurt, anger and desperation has been rising within me for 11 years. Now I'm on the floor bleeding, sobbing my heart out. I'm not trying to kill myself; I just don't know what to do. I just want the pain to go away.

Funny isn't it? When you are hurting so much from all of the emotional pain, you cut yourself. You hurt yourself more so that life won't hurt so much! It makes no sense but bullied kids do it. Boys do it too but they don't talk about it.

## Mum Comes Home

Suddenly I realise Mum and my little brother will be home soon. I go to the bathroom, I clean myself up, I pull down my sleeves and pull myself together. Everything seems normal; Mum will never know. I turn the music on real loud. My mum and brother will have no idea what happened.

A few days later Mum takes me to have some blood tests. I pull my sleeves up for the nurse and that's when Mum sees the scabs on my wrist. When we get home, Mum asks me to explain what happened.

I can't put things into words. I tell her, "I panicked. Everything got to me." I tell Mum, "I'm sorry for what I did."

Mum is sad and disappointed and makes me promise her that I will never cut myself again.

It's almost one year later now and I'm proud to say that I've kept that promise. The bullying continues but I am handling it better.

I would never wish my bullying experience on anyone else.

Tori's email: info@seashell.com.au

## What One Teenager Has Done

Despite years of harassment, Tori has made a stand to stop the bullying. She gives presentations about high school life and bullying to local primary schools and parent groups.

When she was just fourteen, Tori wrote a semi-autobiographical book about bullying called Morgan's Story. She applied for and received a community grant to publish her manuscript. The book was released in 2008.

In September 2008 she was invited to sit on the panel of a public forum on bullying, sharing the stage with a medical doctor, an author and a Deakin University Professor.

In 2009 Tori was interviewed for the ABC Four Corners current affairs program, Bullying in the Playground.

Tired of the negativity and gossip on social networking sites, Tory has created an uplifting Facebook page, Geelong Compliments which invites visitors to post messages of kindness.

If a bullied child like Tori can do all this, what are we doing?

> *Never doubt that a small group of thoughtful, committed citizens can change the world; indeed, it's the only thing that ever has.*
>
> **Margaret Mead**

### Adults Must Act

If your child has cancer, what do you do about it? You cancel other commitments and make medical appointments a priority. You take time off work and seek the best help. You cancel vacations and start treatment as soon as possible. You try anything because your child is at risk

But when a child is being bullied and suffering, what do most parents do? They cancel nothing. They put off meetings with the teachers until it is convenient. They blame the school. In the meantime their child is suffering, minute by minute.

Bullying has become a cancer. Kids are suffering and kids are dying. Parents of children who take their lives say, "If only I had known how serious it was..."

People say, "Someone should do something! The government should do something!" Don't wait for the government! Governments aren't good at taking speedy action. Governments aren't good at inspiring people—that's what individuals do.

Let's get real. Children are not going to fix the bullying problem. Neither is the government! Who is going to tackle it head-on? We are! It is up to parents, adults.

Some parents say, "But bullying is everywhere!" What can you do? Cancer too is everywhere—but we don't just give up. Here's what some people have done:

## Walter Mikac – The Alannah and Madeline Foundation

Walter's wife and two little girls were amongst 35 people shot dead at Australia's worst ever massacre at Port Arthur, Tasmania in 1996. Walter was determined to create something positive from his personal devastation.

Together with a small group of volunteers he founded the Alannah and Madeline Foundation (AMF) to help children who are victims of violence.

The foundation created the Better Buddies program to support primary school children. Students in their first and last year of elementary school buddy up and learn about friendship and caring for others. Younger children feel safer and cared for, and the older children feel valued and respected.

By 2010 over 500 schools had participated in the Better Buddies program. See www.betterbuddies.org.au.

The foundation created the National Centre Against Bullying, see www.ncab.org.au.

The Alannah and Madeline Foundation developed the e-Smart program—a flexible, world-leading system for cybersafety and wellbeing in schools. Over 150 schools participated in the pilot program—and 96% reported that they would recommend it to other schools: www.amf.org.au/eSmart.

The AMF programs have recently been adapted and introduced to Denmark.

# Michele Elliot, OBE

In 1985 Michele Elliot founded "Kidscape"—England's first charity to help abused and bullied children. Today, over 2 million children use Kidscape programs to stay safe.

> **MICHELE'S STORY: KIDSCAPE:** As a Florida psychologist, I worked with abused children. In the 1970s I came to live and work in the UK.
>
> In my new London job, I regularly spoke to community groups about child abuse. After delivering a presentation to say, 200 nurses or doctors, there would be a line of 25 people waiting to tell me their own tragic story. My experience suggested that around ten percent of UK children had suffered sexual abuse at the hands of parents, babysitters, neighbours or relatives. But none of the authorities were doing anything about it!

## "We Have No Problem!"

I organised a meeting with the Department of Health to discuss the problem. I sat down with four government executives who told me, "We don't have a child sex abuse problem in this country! We don't even have a category for it on the risk register!" They told me, "We have between 10 and 20 cases a year in the whole of England".

In my little corner of London, I was seeing 30 cases per week!

I did a survey of 4,000 school children and asked them, "What worries you?" Overwhelmingly the answer was, "I'm scared to go to school." About 40% of the children were somehow affected by bullying.

## "There is No Problem!"

I next met with the National Union of Teachers (NUT). I said, "We have to do something about this bullying problem!" They told me, "Bullying affects only one or two percent of kids. There is no problem".

I was stunned.

I had to do something! I told my husband, Ed, "I am going to quit my job and start a local charity to help abused and bullied children." There were a lot of reasons not to:

- we had no spare money
- we had two young sons, aged two and five
- our family would have to survive on Ed's income only
- I had no office
- I had no idea how to run a charity!

Ed was behind me. All we knew was that we had to help these kids.

I set up my office in a tiny six-foot by eight-foot room at the back of our apartment. It was more like a walk-in closet. I did radio interviews. I wrote to all the newspapers. We were soon swamped with phone calls, 24 hours a day.

I gave presentations to educators and police. We wrote programs for schools. We distributed survival leaflets. I wrote books. We were running out of room and running out of money, when a kind gentleman, John Hadjipateras, suggested that you can't run a charity from a closet. He offered us space—and a photocopier—in his London office. He even donated 10,000 pounds to help Kidscape continue.

Thanks to a growing team of generous and committed people, we have grown into a national organisation.

ZAP

Our one-day course for bullied children, ZAP, has been a revelation. It builds kids' confidence, it teaches them how to interact with other kids. They discover their own self-worth.

For four years we monitored our ZAP results. We had the children complete questionnaires before and after the course and the results showed that ZAP reduced bullying by 80%. We couldn't believe it—so we engaged an independent charities evaluation service to come in and check what we were doing. They confirmed that our ZAP course cuts bullying by 80%.

At Kidscape we train trainers. We produce booklets, posters and training videos. We continue to expand our website www.kidscape.org.

Our message is going global: Kidscape programs have already been translated into Portuguese, Spanish, Greek, Polish and Japanese.

And guess what! The Department of Health is now a major funder of our charity.

What if Michele Elliot had said, "This is not my problem"? What if she had said, "How could one person possibly make a difference?"

Kidscape was named charity of the year in 2000. Michele received an OBE from the Queen in 2008 and she was declared Children and Young People's Champion in 2009.

**In a Nutshell**

Start wherever you can with whatever you have. If you care enough—and if you are committed—good people will support you.

### GenAUSTIN

Originally called the Ophelia Project, GENaustin (Girls Empowerment Network) was created in 1996 by 12 concerned mothers who were each raising adolescent girls in Austin, Texas. They were concerned that so many girls suffer from a poor self-image and poor body-image, poor diet, from drug and alcohol abuse, depression—and bullying.

They created a program to support and guide girls through their teen years. GENAustin runs workshops and conferences and circulates a newsletter. It trains older teens to help younger teens in school.

GENAustin operates in over 50 schools in Central Texas and currently, about 3,500 girls are involved in the program each year.

GENAustin is an example of what happens when parents stop saying, "Someone should do something" and instead say, "WE should do something." See www.genaustin.org.

### Stan Davis

A school guidance counselor Stan began to rethink bullying prevention when he discovered that most of the advice usually given to students doesn't work for them.

At the Bean Elementary School in Maine, USA, Stan built on the work of Dr Dan Olweus and other researchers to create an anti-bullying program that he describes as a partnership between staff and students. Between 1999 and 2006, they reduced bullying at the school by 89%. You can read about the program—and study the data at www.stopbullyingnow.com/beandata.pdf.

Stan's books, *Schools Where Everyone Belongs: Practical Strategies for Reducing Bullying* and *Empowering Bystanders in Bullying Prevention* have become handbooks for schools that are committed to kindness.

Stan was a founder of the International Bullying Prevention Association.

He maintains the website www.stopbullyingnow.com.

**In a Nutshell**

Do your children feel safe in school? If not, what are you doing about it?

## Changing Schools

**PAUL AND MARIA'S STORY:** We enrolled our daughter, Lea, in the most expensive and prestigious school in town because we thought it was the best.

Lea loved her first two years. But in third grade the bullying and the exclusion started. There was name-calling, other girls wouldn't play with her and her former friends wouldn't even talk to her.

Lea began to dread school days and she became more and more unhappy. More and more she spent her lunch hours alone in the library.

We met with Lea's teacher to try to fix the problem. Her teacher asked, "Has Lea been through some kind of trauma somewhere?"

And we said, 'Yes, the trauma is HERE!"

Her teacher suggested that we get Lea involved in team sports like netball, which we did. But the bullying continued and her teacher appeared to lose interest in solving the problem.

We watched our bright little girl descend steadily into a dark hole. We were heartbroken and we felt helpless. Our keen and bubbly little angel had transformed into a shy, depressed little eight-year-old.

We had meetings with the principal—again, for no result. Almost daily, Lea would threaten to leave school during school hours and wander home alone. She begged us, "Send me to any school but here!"

We asked ourselves, "Why are we spending our life savings for such disappointing results? What is the point if your child is miserable every day?" In desperation, we pulled Lea out of her school and enrolled her at our local primary school just down the road.

The change was immediate and profound. On Lea's first day, the teacher and the whole class made her welcome. Two little girls took her by the hand and showed her around the campus. She has been a happy girl ever since.

Now, when we take her to school each day she is greeted by other children. It is not a rich school but it is a kind place. Lea is back to her old self—awake at 5am and ready for school by six. She doesn't need to leave home until eight!

What did we learn? That money won't necessarily buy our children a safer or a better education. All schools are not the same. A miserable child can't learn. Parents must do whatever it takes—and sometimes that means changing schools.

## Schools: What Can Parents Do?

If you are planning to enrol your child in a school, find out what anti-bullying programs the school has in place. The only policy that will work is one that has

the support of the entire staff from the principal down.

If your child is being bullied at school, complain until you get action. The school has a duty to provide a safe learning environment. Your child has a RIGHT to be safe. Sometimes schools deny there is a problem—or blame the target of the bullying. Don't be put off.

Speak to her teacher. If nothing improves, speak to the principal. If nothing improves, keep harassing the principal—and take it further. Contact the school's council or board of governors, speak to your local politician, write to your local newspaper.

If bullying in the school is widespread, collect a petition from parents. Organise a concerned parents group and gather documentation/evidence of bullying.

When you meet with the school, do it in a spirit of cooperation: instead of "You should stop this!" say "How can we help?"

## A Whole School Program

A successful school anti-bullying program is NOT an "add-on accessory" where a teacher pins up some "Zero Tolerance for Bullying" posters and puts a logo on the website.

The foundation of an effective program is this: it's less about how the bullies are punished, and much more about how the whole school thinks.

A number of elements have to come together:

- A PRINCIPAL with the courage to change the school culture—it's called leadership. Like any organisation, it starts at the top.
- A group of TEACHERS who care enough to cooperate in a consistent program incorporating:

  CLEAR RULES. General phrases like *Zero tolerance for bullying* or *Treat everyone with respect* won't do it. Staff and students need to know exactly what is permitted and what is not: eg: NO Teasing—that means name-calling, ridiculing, starting rumours or any other behaviour intended to cause hurt.

  ESCALATING CONSEQUENCES that are the same for all students. In other words, little Billy has to know: "If I hit Mary today, I lose my lunch-hour. If I hit Mary again tomorrow, I lose three lunch-hours—and a letter goes to my parents."
- A group of PARENTS who decide that enough is enough—and then choose to support rather than blame the school.

Schools that reduce bullying teach fairness and tolerance as part of their curriculum: in class, in assemblies, in theatre productions, in the playground. New students are welcomed, differences amongst students are embraced. Through role-playing, bystanders learn how to stand up to bullies. Children who report aggressive behaviour are rewarded for their courage.

These books detail anti-bullying strategies that work:

- *Empowering Bystanders in Bullying Prevention* (2007)
  Stan Davis with Julia Davis (Research Press)
- *Schools Where Everyone Belongs: Practical Strategies in Reducing Bullying* (2007)
  Stan Davis with Julia Davis (Research Press)

- *How to Stop Bullying: A KIDSCAPE Training Guide* (1994)
  Michele Elliot and Jan Kilpatrick (Kidscape)
- *Bullying: A Practical Guide to Coping for Schools* (2002)
  Ed. Michele Elliot (Longman)

**In a Nutshell**
Bullying happens because we let it happen.

# 15. KINDNESS

*Three things in human life are important. The first is to be kind. The second is to be kind. The third is to be kind.*

Henry James

> **J**OANN'S STORY: During my second year of nursing school our professor gave us a quiz. I breezed through the questions until I read the last one: "What is the first name of the woman who cleans the school?"
>
> Surely this was a joke. I had seen the cleaning woman several times, but how would I know her name? I handed in my paper, leaving the last question blank.
>
> Before the class ended, one student asked if the last question would count toward our grade.
>
> "Absolutely", the professor said. "In your careers, you will meet many people. All are significant. They deserve your attention and care, even if all you do is smile and say hello."
>
> I've never forgotten that lesson. I also learned her name was Dorothy.

Isn't this a story for every classroom? If a medical professor can make room for Dorothy the Cleaner amongst the hypertension and the hyperglycemia, what can other teachers do?

We already have enough bullying reports and research papers to stretch to the moon. How much worse does bullying need to get before we teach Kindness alongside Chemistry?

Our best defence against a bullying epidemic is kindness—teaching kindness, not by preaching, but by being kind.

Imagine this: a school where six-year-olds are taught how to make friends—and are taught the importance of playing with everyone. Imagine a school where eight-year-olds practise giving each other compliments and where ten-year-olds write essays about "The Kindest Person I Know". Imagine a school where all children get to make movies about the harmful effects of bullying.

Imagine a curriculum where children study real-life heroes—not the ones that shoot people but the ones that serve people. Imagine a school that holds special weekly assemblies to reward acts of kindness and courage.

Here's the good news: these schools already exist and they have cut bullying in half. Kindness cures but it's not a treatment that you attach like a bandage. You need daily injections—and healing happens from deep inside.

We spend so much time encouraging our children to compete against other kids—and so little time teaching them to be kind. And still, most children grow up to be thoroughly decent and caring.

What magic might happen when we make kindness a priority!

SOURCES

1. Craig, W. and Pepler, D. (2000) Making a Difference in Bullying (LaMarsh Research Programme, Report 60).

2. Hinduja S. and Patchin J. (2009) Bullying Beyond the Schoolyard Corwin Press p. 14

3. Walk Tall, composer Don Wayne, permission requested

4. Olweus, D. (1993) Bullying at School Blackwell Publishing p.34

5. Davis S. and Davis J. (2007) Schools Where Everyone Belongs Research Press p.13

6. Dellasega C. and Nixon C. (2003) Girl Wars Simon and Schuster p.8

7. Davis S. and Davis J. (2007) Schools Where Everyone Belongs Research Press p. 24

8. Davis S. and Davis J. (2007) Empowering Bystanders in Bullying Prevention Research Press p. 1-2

9. Shaw R. The Epidemic (2003) Harper Collins, permission requested.

10. Davis S. and Davis J. (2007) Empowering Bystanders in Bullying Prevention Research Press p. 111

# Andrew Matthews: Speaker

Andrew Matthews speaks to conferences worldwide.

He has addressed over a thousand international corporations on five continents.

Andrew speaks to banks, hospitals, government institutions, IT corporations, prisons and he has addressed more than 500 universities and schools around the world.

Andrew's topics include:

- attitude
- dealing with disasters
- embracing change
- life/ work balance
- prosperity and success
- bullying

To engage Andrew:

- email: info@seashell.com.au
- tel: +61 740 556 966
- www.andrewmatthews.com

## Bullied People Speak...

- *"When everybody stands and watches, you feel you deserve it."*

- *"Here it is, 30 years since we moved away from the bully and he still controls my life!"*

- *"I can remember every word those fiends said. I've been hearing their bullying jeers all my life."*

- *"Grandmother, please live a long life. Father, thank you for the trip to Australia. Mother, thank you for the delicious meals. I wanted to live longer, but... "*

- *"I don't want to end my life but it is the only way to end the pain."*

How did bullying get out of control? Because most of us are BYSTANDERS—we know bullying is happening and we do nothing.

*Stop the Bullying* is about action we can all take—and must take.